ADRIANA LUNA CARLOS
Editor-In-Chief, Designer
and Co-Founder

HANNA OLIVAS
Managing Editor
& Co-Founder

NICOLE CURTIS
Director of the SRS
Magazine Division

VITALITY DIGEST

**ADVERTISING
OPPORTUNITIES**
Info@SheRisesStudios.com

SHE RISES
STUDIOS

CONTACT US
SheRisesStudios@gmail.com
www.SheRisesStudios.com

**VITALITY DIGEST MAGAZINE
FEBRUARY 2025**

www.SheRisesStudios.com

LETTER FROM THE EDITORS

Dear Readers,

Welcome to the February 2025 edition of Vitality Digest Magazine! As the year draws to a close, we are thrilled to bring you an issue brimming with inspiration, empowerment, and tools to help you embrace a life of Heart and Harmony. This month, our cover star, the phenomenal Hunyah Irfan, graces our pages with her unique blend of creativity and passion. As a content creator and facilitator of the HunyahTravels YouTube channel, she invites us on an extraordinary journey through food, travel, and meaningful connection.

In this edition, we dive deep into prioritizing health, wellness, and self-love —the foundation of a life well-lived. From practical tips to embrace these pillars to heartfelt stories that remind us of the importance of balance, every page is crafted to inspire and energize. Whether you're discovering wellness practices that spark joy or exploring the transformative power of self-care, this issue is a treasure trove of insights.

We're also thrilled to share an exciting announcement: the She Wins Women's Network is launching in 2025! This membership opportunity is designed to establish growth, collaboration, and empowerment for women everywhere. Details can be found inside, so don't miss your chance to be part of this incredible community.

As always, we thank you for joining us on this journey to vitality. Together, let's embrace the beauty of balance and the power of connection. Here's to a life filled with Heart and Harmony!

Warm regards,

Adriana Luna Carlos and Hanna Olivas
Editors of Vitality Digest Magazine

FENIX TV

SHE RISES
S T U D I O S

EMPOWER**HER**
CONTENT DAY

at

Elevate Your Brand Through Creative And Impactful Content!

EmpowerHer Content Day equips attendees with the tools and knowledge needed to craft compelling content for social media, podcasts, and videos.

FEBRUARY 22, 2025

TOTAL ACCESS TICKET: $127

WWW.SHERISESSTUDIOS.COM

BALANCING ART, LIFE, AND ADVOCACY: HUNYAH IRFAN'S CREATIVE VISION AND JOURNEY TO EMPOWERMENT

Hunyah Irfan's journey into the world of content creation, spoken word poetry, and facilitation is a story of resilience, passion, and self-discovery. Raised in Brampton, Ontario, she has always been drawn to creative expression. Inspired by her childhood fascination with celebrities, Hunyah's journey took a unique turn as she found herself captivated by food, travel, and the art of storytelling. As a content creator, Hunyah combines these passions to build an online presence that offers much more than just entertainment—her platform serves as a space for inspiration, learning, and authenticity.

Hunyah's YouTube channel, HunyahTravels, started almost serendipitously in the year before the COVID-19 pandemic. After a traumatic accident in her twenties and struggling to find a stable job despite various attempts in retail, Hunyah faced a period of uncertainty. She even pursued employment training, but found that it didn't align with her true passions. *"I thought, why not do something I am passionate about?"* Hunyah recalls. It was this desire to turn her love for food and travel into something meaningful that sparked the creation of HunyahTravels. Initially, the channel began as a space for small training programs during the lockdown, such as graphic design, cultural sensitivity, and cooking. These programs not only honed her skills in cooking and design but also laid the foundation for her growth as a facilitator.

Six years later, Hunyah has cultivated a loyal community of 160 subscribers on YouTube, alongside a growing Instagram following of 2,000. While her channel is still in its early stages compared to some of the industry giants, Hunyah's raw and authentic approach to content creation has set her apart.

"I don't edit a lot in my videos. Most of what you see is real and unfiltered, whether it's the places I visit or the food I review," she explains. This authenticity resonates with viewers, drawing them into her journey rather than just presenting them with polished content.

What sets HunyahTravels apart from other food and travel channels is its deeply personal touch. From humble beginnings, the channel has evolved, with each new project growing bigger and more ambitious than the last. Hunyah's evolution as a content creator is not only reflected in her videos but in the constant learning and self-improvement that she shares with her audience.

Spoken word poetry has always been an integral part of Hunyah's creative expression.

HunyahTravels
Youtube Channel
HUNYAH IRFAN

offical hunyahtravels

HunyahTravels1

HunyahTravels1

hunyahtravels@gmail.com

As a child, she dabbled in poetry in her free time, using it as a means to process her thoughts and emotions. Over time, poetry became a deeper form of communication for her, especially as she began exploring themes of self-burnout, depression, and personal struggle. *"Sometimes the most depressing poems are the best,"* Hunyah muses, acknowledging that the weight of difficult experiences often yields the most powerful creative work.

Her poetry serves as a form of catharsis, not only for herself but for others who may be navigating similar emotions. Through her spoken word, Hunyah shares raw and vulnerable pieces that shed light on mental health struggles, offering both solace and solidarity to those who listen. Her poetry is not just an artistic expression—it's a tool for healing and understanding.

In addition to being a content creator and spoken word artist, Hunyah's role as a facilitator plays a significant part in her career. Her time teaching disabled arts at Western University shaped her perspective on the importance of inclusivity and the diversity of human experiences. Being the youngest facilitator in the group, Hunyah learned that not all disabilities are the same. *"You can be a well-known artist, but everyone is dealing with something,"* she reflects. This realization informed her approach as a facilitator—ensuring that every participant is respected, heard, and given the time and space to flourish.

Her experience as a facilitator also extends to hosting virtual open mics. What she enjoys most about these events is the opportunity to listen to others' poetry and provide them with a platform to share their stories. Creating a welcoming space for participants is a priority for Hunyah, as she believes that the power of poetry lies in its ability to connect people and give voice to experiences that may otherwise go unheard.

Hunyah's upbringing in Brampton, Ontario, has been pivotal in shaping her creative vision. Growing up in the Region of Peel, she spent her teenage years frequently visiting Bramalea City Center, an experience that connected her to both Mississauga and Brampton. Hunyah credits her mother's unwavering support for her success, always encouraging her to strive for greatness and helping her stay focused on her goals. Additionally, her long-distance cousin, who inspired her to try new things, has had a profound influence on Hunyah's creative journey.

Her travel experiences also play a major role in her artistic development. As a teenager, Hunyah would visit New York City every summer, a place she feels deeply connected to. These visits exposed her to different cultures, broadening her creative perspective. *"I know New York really well,"* she says, noting how travel has shaped her worldview and influenced her work.

Brampton's vibrant artist community also plays a crucial role in her creative expression. The city has a diverse and active arts scene, offering something for everyone. For Hunyah, this community serves as both a source of inspiration and a reminder that the creative possibilities are endless.

Hunyah's journey has not been without its challenges. Throughout her career, she has faced negativity and rumors, particularly from her extended family. Despite these obstacles, she remains undeterred. *"I try to ignore these things and move on,"* she says, emphasizing her resilience in the face of adversity. Time management and comparison, especially within the South Asian community, have also presented hurdles. Yet, Hunyah has learned to navigate these challenges, using her passion and determination to fuel her progress.

For those aspiring to follow a similar path, Hunyah's advice is simple yet profound: *"Write about your passion. Be honest in your work. And listen to people's stories."* She encourages aspiring content creators, poets, and facilitators to stay true to themselves, create meaningful content, and take the time to enjoy the journey. *"Everyone has a disability, and we should never judge others for theirs,"* she adds, reminding creators to embrace their own vulnerabilities and those of others.

Hunyah Irfan's story is a testament to the power of passion, perseverance, and the willingness to learn. From her humble beginnings as a content creator to her growing influence as a spoken word artist and facilitator, Hunyah continues to inspire those around her. Through her work, she is not only creating content but cultivating a community of like-minded individuals who share her love for self-expression, growth, and connection.

CONNECT WITH HUNYAH

www.linktr.ee/Hunyah_Travels
www.youtube.com/@officalhunyahtravels1
www.linkedin.com/in/hunyah-irfan-blogger351
Instagram: @officalhunyahtravels, @hunyah22

HEART MOM AND NURSE: A STORY OF STRENGTH AND OVERCOMING CHALLENGES AS A PARENT

by Sarah Michelle Boes, MSN, APRN, FNP-BC

As a nurse practitioner, heart month used to be a moment where I would pause to reflect on cardiovascular health and wear red to support the cause. I was merely a cog in the wheel to the bigger heart month picture as it related to my patients at the time. I had only a small glimpse into what heart month even meant. However, heart month has since taken on new meaning and purpose for me since the birth of my daughter, Meadow. Heart month is now a time of advocacy, love and dedication for my daughter's future and those like her.

Meadow was unexpectedly born with a combination of four different heart defects known as Tetralogy of Fallot with Pulmonary Atresia. This is a fancy way of saying that she was missing critical pieces of her heart and had holes in places they did not belong when she was born. Her first major heart surgery occurred at only 6 days old, with her palliative full repair being completed at 4 months old. This is not the end of her heart story though or even close - it is only the beginning of a lifetime of care she will need to simply survive.

There is no cure for congenital heart disease, despite it being the most common birth defect. There is a diagnosis of congenital heart disease quite literally every 15 minutes as 1 in 100 babies are born with a heart defect. Meadow is why heart month is so important to me. That is because her care, and the care of so many children like her, is simply palliative. Palliative is a hard word to stomach as a parent because it means there is no cure, just a band aid until the next surgery. There is no grand fix to her native heart, and instead she faces a lifetime of several more open heart surgeries unless medical advancements can catch up to her needs. I hope for this innovation each and every day, and will do anything I can to support it.

I envision a different future for children like Meadow, which is why advocacy during heart month (and truly through the entirety of the year too) is now front and center in my life.

Increasing awareness leads to increased funding and research so that these children can live longer, healthier lives. It's only been in recent years that there are now more adults living with congenital heart disease than children, which is so beautiful. While we are now getting them to adulthood though, there is so much more work to be done. Heart month shines a spotlight on these special children so that we can pave the path to the future for them.

We change the future by focusing on the present - so share these statistics with those you know. Because Meadow's scar is tucked neatly away in most of her clothes, most people would never know the surgeries she has had or will continue to have in the future. Awareness is the key for moving forward into this future where hearts are a part of the focus. It is very likely that if you do not know someone with a congenital heart defect, you will soon because they are just that prevalent.

I share a small piece of her story here with you today because I truly believe her zipper scar is where her light shines through the most. Her heart defects are not all of her by any means, but her imperfect heart changes the trajectory of her entire life moving forward. I hope in this heart month you will spend a small moment with me in her story and consider how your increased awareness can change the world she lives in.

CONNECT WITH SARAH

www.sarahmichelleboes.com
www.instagram.com/sarahmichellenp/?hl=en
www.linkedin.com/in/sarah-michelle-287616232

THE MEDICINE TO HEAL

by Debra Hillard

I have story upon story recounting my experiences with medicine of all kinds. Doctors, tests, procedures, all offered as the *"cure"* for what was ailing me. Nothing worked. It began very early on in my life, strange maladies that no one could pin down, but so many thought they had the fix for. Many said what ailed me was "all in my head" and I needed a shrink. The shrinks said that it was physical and what I needed was the right *"medicine"*, but no one seemed to know what that medicine was.

With no precedent to follow, I blindly trusted the so called experts, only to pile on more and more symptoms and medications, some with symptoms worse than the original they were supposed to cure. What was not apparent to me all those years ago was that modern medicine couldn't cure what ailed me and that there was a *"medicine"* much more potent than any they had to offer. I was unaware of the real cause of my ills, the fear that permeated every moment of my waking and sleeping life.

Fast forward 6 decades.

Now I know what medicine really is, the potent kind that treats the root of illness.

Though it might sound simple and easy to dismiss, I want to preface this by saying that I dismissed this for far too long out of arrogance and ignorance. I wouldn't admit that it was this simple. I didn't say easy....I said simple.

Healing happens in the presence of truth, bathed in love. Deep, dark, often painful truth brought into the light to be seen and lovingly walked through until the darkness and the light play off one another in a new dance.

How could that be? I was sure it had to be more complex than that. But what I hadn't identified was what true love really was and what it was going to take to feel worthy of it. This is an unconditional love that required me to forgive myself first and make peace with my own humanity, my frailties and flaws.

Will love heal a damaged spine or arthritic hands? Will it repair the damage done to organs and systems in my body affected by years of stress? I don't know, but what I do know is that all of the medicine and procedures and tests that doctors have offered so far have only made things worse.

What do I have to lose by treating myself with love?

How does this translate into real life action? It means that when we create our lives, they must be created with love as the main ingredient. We must choose the elements that go into our lives because we love them. If something doesn't light you up, it doesn't belong in your life. Choose things out of passion, delight, and just because they bring you joy. The elements that make up your life have to be true to your soul, and they don't have to make sense to anyone else.

The medicine to heal is the same medicine I need to create. It is made from the kind of love that knows no bounds and has no judgement. It has no side effects other than fulfillment, delight and joy. It doesn't need a doctor's prescription or insurance approval. And it doesn't cost anything except the courage and willingness to administer it to myself. This is not a medicine that anyone else can give me. I am the healer here. So are you. Create the painting of your life from what you love.

ROSITA PEREZ: A VOICE OF RESILIENCE AND EMPOWERMENT FOR MIDLIFE WOMEN

Rosita Perez embodies the essence of transformation, strength, and joy. After a lifetime of navigating pain, self-doubt, and reinvention, she now stands as a beacon of hope for midlife women seeking purpose and authenticity. Fueled by her unwavering faith and practical tools, Rosita overcame a childhood filled with limiting beliefs and emerged as a fierce advocate and Mindset Coach for women in their midlife journey.

Her story, shaped by profound losses, divorce, and resilience, underscores the transformative power of forgiveness and healing. In her chapter, Rising from the Ashes, featured in the book She Stands Strong, Rosita offers a compelling testament to the beauty and strength found in embracing your true self. Her message to midlife women is clear: It's never too late to step boldly into the life you were meant to live. You can live UNSTOPPABLE.

Through her personal journey, Rosita shares six transformative insights that drive her forward and inspire others:

1. Personal Healing and Transformation
Rosita highlights the power of prioritizing yourself and investing in deep inner healing. By cultivating self-love and doing the necessary work to address pain, she turned her life around. Her story reminds us that transformation is possible at any age, especially when guided by faith and perseverance.

2. Embracing Forgiveness for Family Healing
Rosita's journey includes breaking generational cycles of silence and unhealthy behaviors. Through prayer, therapy, and mutual respect, she and her daughter are rewriting their family's narrative. Her experience offers a roadmap to reconciliation and healing, proving that forgiveness can pave the way for deeper connections.

3. Building a Relationship with God and Faith
Faith has been Rosita's anchor through life's storms. From overcoming abusive relationships to enduring the pain of divorce, her spiritual strength and practical tools have provided clarity and resilience. She demonstrates how a relationship with God can help rebuild your life with purpose.

4. Rising from Heartache with Purpose
Every painful experience—from the betrayal in her marriages to the loss of her mother—became an opportunity for reinvention. Rosita's story illustrates that even in the darkest moments, hope remains. With faith and action, renewal is always within reach.

5. Living Authentically at Midlife
Rosita shed the weight of self-doubt and fear to embrace her authentic self. By stepping into her power, she transformed her life and found her calling as a Mindset Coach. Today, she helps women navigate midlife challenges, reclaim their joy, and rediscover their purpose.

6. A Legacy of Love and Empowerment
As a mother and grandmother, Rosita is determined to break free from limiting beliefs and pass on lessons of self-worth, love, and boundaries. She empowers other women to do the same, showing that midlife can be a time of reinvention, connection, and profound purpose.

Rosita's journey would not have been possible without her faith in God and the unwavering support of her community of family and friends.

As a Mindset Coach, Rosita draws from her experiences of overcoming cultural norms, family expectations, and personal grief. She combines Christian principles with actionable strategies to help women conquer self-doubt, rediscover their voices, and boldly step into their true identities. Her mission is to guide women toward cultivating an unstoppable mindset and reclaiming their lives.

Rosita reminds us: *"Your journey is far from over—it's just beginning. You hold the wisdom of experience and the power to redefine your future."*

Believe it ~ Speak it ~ Be it!

CONNECT WITH ROSITA
www.movingforwardforlife.com
www.facebook.com/rositamovingforwardforlife
www.youtube.com/@unstoppablemidlife

EMPOWERING FAMILIES THROUGH HEALTH EDUCATION

by Sheree Wertz

Sheree Wertz is a dedicated dental hygienist and myofunctional therapist whose mission is to improve the health and well-being of families through education and personalized care. With over a decade of experience in the dental field, Sheree has witnessed firsthand the significant impact of oral health on overall wellness. Her journey led her to specialize in myofunctional therapy, where she focuses on the interconnectedness of breathing, sleep, and oral function.

Sheree's commitment to health education is driven by her belief that knowledge is power. *"Empowerment begins with education,"* she often says, emphasizing the importance of understanding health issues to make informed decisions. Her approach combines personalized care with practical strategies that families can easily implement in their daily lives. By educating families about the significance of oral health, Sheree empowers them to prioritize their health and make proactive choices.

In her chapter for Plan A Life You Love, Sheree introduces her innovative SHIFT method, which stands for Sleep, Habit, Intake, Function, and Time. This holistic approach helps families improve their health through simple habit adjustments. By addressing issues related to oral function and overall wellness, Sheree provides families with the tools they need to embrace a healthier lifestyle. She shares actionable tips for improving sleep quality, developing healthy eating habits, and optimizing oral function to enhance overall well-being.

Sheree's dedication to education extends beyond her practice. She offers workshops and community outreach programs aimed at promoting awareness about the significance of oral health and its connection to overall well-being. Through engaging presentations and interactive discussions, Sheree inspires families to take charge of their health and cultivate a culture of wellness. Her passion for teaching is evident, and she is committed to making a positive impact on the communities she serves.

Through her compassionate approach and commitment to education, Sheree Wertz is making a significant impact on the lives of families. Her belief in the power of informed choices encourages individuals to take control of their health and thrive. By empowering families to prioritize their well-being, Sheree is transforming lives and fostering a healthier future for generations to come.

CONNECT WITH SHEREE

www.linkedin.com/in/sheree-wertz-43b71a46
www.facebook.com/groups/healthymouthmoms
www.instagram.com/dental_hygiene_411
www.shereewertz.com
www.dentalhygiene411.com

HOW TO PRIORITIZE HEALTH AND HAPPINESS BY TREATING SLEEP APNEA

by Andres Moran - Co-Founder and CEO of Complete Sleep

I suffocated in my sleep over 160 times every single night, as I learned when I was diagnosed with sleep apnea. The news came as somewhat of a relief because it explained the past few years of daily fatigue and limited patience.

That relief was short-lived when the only solution my doctor suggested to me was a CPAP machine. Despite my verbalizing that I refused to sleep with a CPAP, the doctor continued to force it upon me as my best option. Eventually, they mentioned that a custom night guard could also improve my apnea, but that they couldn't help me get one. I then had to spend months and considerable effort getting one of these night guards, and it still cost me a fortune!

My struggles in treating my own sleep apnea led me to launch Complete Sleep. Let's bring the entire process under one roof – from education, to home sleep testing, to custom night guard procurement, to insurance billing, to continued support.

Frankly, treating sleep apnea successfully can have a transformative impact on your life, and I know this from personal experience. It might feel daunting, but it is actually easily possible!

By now it's well known that mental and physical health are directly linked to sleep. In fact, getting good quality sleep can boost your brain performance, your overall mood, your immune system, and more. Sleep apnea makes it literally impossible to get quality sleep. Therefore, treating sleep apnea can help you feel more present and engaged, both at work and at home with friends and family. Anyone who's a parent understands the need to have enough energy to take care of kids every day.

Rather than spending countless hours of effort to treat sleep apnea— which can be lonely, anxiety-inducing, and overwhelming— people can now get to an effective solution to sleep apnea with Complete Sleep in a matter of 2-3 weeks from home. And that makes people feel confident and gives them peace of mind.

We've done everything to eliminate the barriers that stand in your way to quality sleep. We've turned the mountain into a molehill.

Healthy sleep is about sleep quality, meaning that you get uninterrupted and refreshing sleep, not just quantity of sleep. And, it's about having a consistent sleep schedule. Easier said than done.

Create a calm bedroom environment for yourself: no TV, no screens, nice lighting, and comfortable bedding. You could try meditating before bedtime, reading a favorite book, listening to music, or using calming essential oils such as lavender. A nice cup of herbal tea can also help create a gentle bedtime routine, too. Get blackout blinds or curtains to keep the room dark, and make sure it's at a cool temperature.

If possible, try to go to bed and wake up around the same time each day to keep up a consistent schedule of restorative sleep, even on weekends.

The legacy treatment for sleep apnea can take 6 months. It's a convoluted path to treatment, involving many consults and appointments with in-person specialists and providers, waitlists, months between appointments, and countless hours of wasted time. However, our solution is a single point of coordination done entirely from home in 3 weeks.

We want people to know that they don't have to settle for their mother's or grandmother's method of treating sleep apnea. There's a new way to do it, and dare I say the process may even be delightful if handled by a modern solution provider!

CONNECT WITH ANDRES

www.mycompletesleep.com
www.instagram.com/getcompletesleep
www.linkedin.com/company/complete-sleep

BREAKING CHAINS: FROM EVENT SUCCESS TO ADDICTION AND BACK

by Connie Paglianiti

I spent over 40 years in the high-pressure world of event management, creating unforgettable experiences with celebrities like Susan Sarandon, Sophia Loren, Jane Seymour and Goldie Hawn. I orchestrated everything from intimate charity galas to large-scale festivals for thousands. My work earned state awards in Victoria, including for the La Dolce Italia Carnevale Masquerade Ball, a finalist for Best New Event. It was a glamorous, fast-paced life. But behind the scenes, I was battling a personal struggle far darker than anyone could have imagined.

From the Pinnacle of Success to Addiction

It all started when a business deal went horribly wrong. I was deceived by someone I trusted, and in an attempt to recover my losses, I turned to gambling. What began as a means to regain control soon spiraled into a destructive addiction. My life, once defined by successful events and accolades, began to unravel.

The losses piled up, not just financially, but emotionally and spiritually. I made choices I deeply regret, choices that ultimately landed me in prison for two and a half years. The shame, guilt, and fear of losing everything I had built were suffocating. When I was released, I isolated myself, spending another two and a half years hiding from the world, convinced my life and career were over.

Rebuilding from the Ashes

Recovery from addiction is never easy, and my journey was no exception. It required humility, vulnerability, and a willingness to face the damage I had done—not just to my life, but to those who trusted me. Through therapy, support groups, and the strength of the people around me, I started to rebuild.

One of the most powerful lessons I learned is that addiction doesn't discriminate. It can take hold of anyone, no matter how successful or in control they may seem. But recovery is possible, and it's worth every moment of struggle. Today, I use my experience to raise awareness about gambling addiction and the importance of breaking the stigma surrounding it.

A New Purpose

In returning to the world of event management, I found a renewed sense of purpose. My career had always been about creating experiences, but now it was about more than just the event itself. It became a platform to champion causes, inspire change, and give back to the communities that supported me.

As a speaker for Gambler's Help and their ReSPIN Program, I share my story to help others avoid the same pitfalls. I want to show people that no matter how far you've fallen, there's always a way back. My story is one of redemption and resilience, and if it can help even one person, it's worth sharing.

I've also channelled my passion for events into educating others. I've written eBooks on event management and developed online courses to train the next generation of event managers. My goal is not just to teach the logistics of running events but to instil the importance of ethics, sustainability, and resilience.

Looking Forward

It's been a long road from award-winning event management to addiction and recovery. The journey has taught me the value of vulnerability, second chances, and self-compassion. I want my story to be a testament to the fact that no matter how deep the fall, you can rise again.

Today, I'm proud of the work I've done and the person I've become. I continue to manage events, speak about addiction recovery, and share my story of resilience.

If my experiences can offer hope and inspiration to others, then every challenge I faced was worth it.

CONNECT WITH CONNIE

www.conniepaglianiti.com
www.linkedin.com/in/conniepaglianiti
www.instagram.com/conniempaglianiti
www.facebook.com/ConniePaglianiti
www.facebook.com/profile.php?id=61560347468477

EMPOWERING MOTHERHOOD THROUGH PEER-TO-PEER MENTORING: A NEW PATH TO PERSONAL AND PROFESSIONAL GROWTH

by Ana Martinez RN

In the intricate dance of balancing career ambitions and the demands of motherhood, finding support and guidance can be a game-changer. This is where peer-to-peer mentoring comes in—a dynamic and transformative approach to personal and professional development that is particularly empowering for mothers. Embracing a peer-to-peer mentor not only fosters growth and confidence, but also enriches the motherhood experience in ways that are both practical and emotionally fulfilling.

1. Fostering a Supportive Sisterhood to Build a Legacy of Empowerment

One of the most remarkable benefits of peer-to-peer mentoring for mothers is the creation of a nurturing and supportive sisterhood which creates a ripple effect of empowerment. This supportive network provides a safe space for sharing struggles, celebrating successes, and exchanging practical advice, helping to alleviate the isolation and loneliness that can sometimes accompany motherhood. Additionally, unlike traditional mentoring relationships where the mentor may be significantly more experienced, peer-to-peer mentoring is grounded in shared experiences and mutual understanding. When mothers connect with peers who are navigating similar challenges, they form a bond of empathy and solidarity. By supporting one another, mothers contribute to a culture of mutual respect and encouragement that extends beyond their immediate circles. As mothers uplift and inspire each other, they create a stronger, more supportive village that benefits everyone involved.

2. Promoting Work-Life Harmony and Continuous Mutual Learning, Growth, and Development

The quest for work-life balance is a challenge for mothers striving to excel in both their personal and professional lives. In a peer-to-peer mentoring relationship, growth is a two-way street and continuous learning is central to effective peer-to-peer mentoring. A unique advantage in this area is by facilitating the exchange of strategies and solutions that are tailored to the realities of motherhood. Through

candid conversations with peers who have faced similar dilemmas, mothers can gain valuable insights into effective time management, prioritization, and self-care techniques helping them find practical solutions but also fostering a sense of shared understanding and encouragement. This mutual exchange of ideas and feedback can lead to personal and professional development that is both relevant and impactful. Whether it's refining leadership skills, exploring career opportunities, or navigating the complexities of parenting, peer mentors offer fresh perspectives and innovative approaches that can inspire and empower mothers to achieve their goals.

3. Strengthening Confidence and Resilience

Motherhood and career pursuits are filled with moments of doubt and challenge. A peer-to-peer mentor is a powerful ally in building confidence and resilience. By sharing their own experiences and strategies for overcoming obstacles, peer mentors provide practical advice and emotional support that can bolster a mother's self-assurance. This shared journey not only helps in navigating current challenges but also instills a greater sense of resilience and empowerment, allowing mothers to approach both their personal and professional lives with renewed vigor and optimism,

In conclusion, the benefits of hiring a peer-to-peer mentor for mothers are both profound and multifaceted. From fostering a supportive sisterhood to promoting work-life harmony, peer-to-peer mentoring offers a unique and empowering pathway to personal and professional growth. By embracing this collaborative approach, mothers can navigate the complexities of their roles with greater confidence, resilience, and success. In the journey of motherhood and career development, peer-to-peer mentoring stands out as a powerful tool for unlocking potential and creating a fulfilling and balanced life.

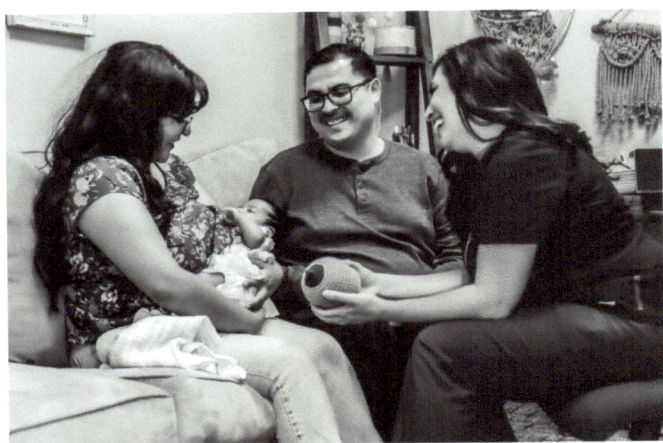

CONNECT WITH ANA

www.ANewAdventureLV.com
www.calendly.com/anamlv/30min
www.facebook.com/anarnclc
www.instagram.com/anam.rnclc
www.linkedin.com/in/anamlv

KEEPING A POSITIVE MINDSET IN A TOPSY-TURVY WORLD

by Ginny Jones

In a world that often feels like a whirlwind of chaos and uncertainty, maintaining a positive mindset can be a powerful tool for navigating the ups and downs of life. Amidst the topsy-turvy nature of the world, it is essential to cultivate a sense of optimism and resilience to counter the challenges that come our way. Here are some valuable insights and practical tips to help you keep a positive mindset and steer clear of anxiety and stress.

Positive affirmations are a potent way to start your day on the right note. By repeating positive statements to yourself, you can reframe your thoughts and focus on the good in every situation. Affirmations like *"I am capable of overcoming any obstacle"* or *"I choose peace and positivity in all aspects of my life"* can help set the tone for a day filled with optimism and resilience.

One effective strategy to maintain a positive mindset is to practice gratitude daily. Take a few moments each day to reflect on the things you are grateful for, whether it's the support of loved ones, a beautiful sunrise, or simply the gift of a new day. Cultivating a mindset of gratitude can shift your focus from what is lacking to what is abundant in your life, fostering a sense of contentment and positivity.

Another essential aspect of keeping a positive mindset is to prioritize self-care. Engaging in activities that nurture your body, mind, and soul can significantly impact your overall well-being. Whether it's taking a leisurely walk in nature, practicing yoga, or indulging in a relaxing bath, make time for self-care rituals that rejuvenate and replenish your energy.

Mindfulness and meditation are powerful tools for managing anxiety and stress. By practicing mindfulness, you can bring your attention to the present moment and cultivate a sense of calm amidst the chaos. Simple breathing exercises and guided meditations can help you center yourself and let go of worries about the past or future, allowing you to focus on the here and now.

Setting boundaries and learning to say no are crucial aspects of maintaining a positive mindset. It's okay to prioritize your well-being and decline commitments that overwhelm you. By establishing boundaries and honoring your needs, you can create a sense of balance and harmony in your life, reducing stress and promoting a positive outlook.

Finding joy in the little things and embracing a sense of humor can also contribute to a positive mindset. Laughter is truly therapeutic and can help you navigate challenging situations with grace and resilience. Surround yourself with people who uplift and inspire you, and don't be afraid to seek support when needed.

In conclusion, keeping a positive mindset in a topsy-turvy world is a continuous journey that requires practice, patience, and self-compassion. By incorporating positive affirmations, practicing gratitude, prioritizing self-care, embracing mindfulness, setting boundaries, and finding joy in everyday moments, you can cultivate a resilient and optimistic outlook on life. Remember, you have the power to choose how you respond to life's challenges – choose positivity, choose resilience, and choose self-care.

I hope this helps you.

Much Love,
Ginny
www.ginnyjoneshealer.com

CONNECT WITH GINNY

www.ginnyjoneshealer.com
www.facebook.com/ginny.jonesartist
www.instagram.com/ginnyintuitiveservices
www.linkedin.com/in/virginia-ginny-jones-2b411236

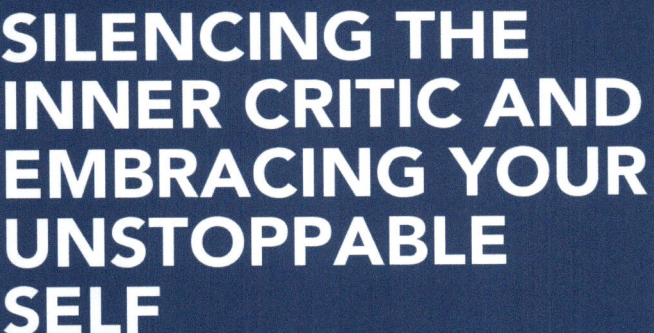

SILENCING THE INNER CRITIC AND EMBRACING YOUR UNSTOPPABLE SELF

by Dr. Shade Kolade

Have you ever stood on the edge of an opportunity, your heart pounding as that inner voice whispers, *"What if I'm not good enough?"* That voice—the relentless critic within—has a way of holding us back, turning our potential into hesitation and our dreams into distant possibilities.

For many women, self-doubt isn't fleeting; it's a persistent inner voice shaped by societal expectations, gender biases, and personal criticism. But here's the truth: while common, it doesn't have to define us.

Understanding Self-Doubt: The Hidden Challenge

Self-doubt often hides behind a mask of humility or realism, but it can sabotage even the most capable among us. For many, it manifests as imposter syndrome—the belief that despite evidence of success, you're a fraud waiting to be exposed.

Where does this self-doubt come from?

- **Societal Expectations:** Gender stereotypes that undervalue women's abilities.
- **Past Experiences:** Lingering criticism or failures that undermine confidence.
- **Unrealistic Comparisons:** Measuring yourself against unattainable standards.
- **Representation Gaps:** A lack of visible role models in leadership.

The good news? Self-doubt thrives in silence, and by acknowledging and addressing it, you can take the first step toward freedom.

Three Strategies to Silence Self-Doubt
1. Reframe Your Inner Narrative
Your thoughts shape your reality. When self-doubt surfaces, counter it with empowering beliefs:

- Replace *"I'm not good enough"* with *"I'm learning and growing every day."*
- Acknowledge that perfection is a myth—progress matters more than flawlessness.
- Treat yourself with the same compassion you'd offer a close friend.

2. Build a Support Network
You don't have to go it alone. Surround yourself with people who uplift and inspire you:

- Seek mentors who challenge and guide you.
- Connect with like-minded women who share your journey.
- Lean on a circle of allies who celebrate your victories and offer honest feedback.

3. Embrace Growth as a Journey
Turn self-doubt into fuel for development:

- View challenges as opportunities to learn, not as obstacles to avoid.
- Document your achievements in a *"success journal"* to remind yourself of your progress.
- Invest in workshops, courses, and skill-building activities that build confidence.

Sarah's Story
Sarah, a working mother of two, struggled to balance her career, family, and personal goals. Despite her accomplishments, she constantly questioned whether she was doing enough at work or home.

Determined to silence her inner critic, she started small, and kept a journal of daily wins, from professional achievements to moments of gratitude with her kids. With her mentor's guidance, Sarah applied for a leadership role she once felt unqualified for. To her surprise, she not only got the position but thrived, leading her team with confidence. Her journal of wins became a daily reminder of her growth.

Your Path to Empowerment
What would your life look like if you silenced your inner critic? Imagine the opportunities you could seize and the dreams you could bring to life.

Start today with these simple steps:

- **Pinpoint a Doubt:** Identify an area where self-doubt holds you back.
- **Log Your Wins:** Create an *"evidence list"* of your accomplishments, big and small.
- **Affirm Your Worth:** Practice daily affirmations like *"I am capable, worthy, and enough."*
- **Take Action:** Pick one area today where doubt holds you back—whether it's asking for a promotion, speaking up in a meeting, or pursuing a personal goal—and take a single bold step toward it. The journey begins with action.

The Journey to Your Unstoppable Self
Self-doubt isn't your story—it's just a chapter. Every woman you admire has faced that inner critic and chosen to rise above it. The same power resides within you. By silencing the critic and embracing your unstoppable self, you open doors to opportunities, joy, and success.

As Eleanor Roosevelt once said, *'You gain strength, courage, and confidence by every experience in which you stop to look fear in the face. You must do the thing you think you cannot do.'* Why not start today?

MAKE THE CHANGE, BE THE CHANGE: 5 STEPS TO UNLOCK PERSONAL SUCCESS IN 2025

by Paula C. Lamb

We are well into the New Year, and I'm curious—have you set any New Year's resolutions? How is it going? Personally, I've never been one for resolutions. At this current time, I prefer to set intentions because they focus on what you want to become and the qualities you wish to embody, rather than a specific outcome. Intentions are about creating a mindset, direction, and energy you want to cultivate in your life. I believe true personal success begins with who we are being and how we show up in the world.

Success in any given year isn't just about setting goals and intentions; it's also about embracing change, taking action, and committing to self-transformation. If you haven't set a goal or intention for 2025, I invite you to join me in focusing on cultivating a deeper sense of transformation this year and beyond. As Gary Goodridge once said, *"Don't strive to be well-known; strive to be worth knowing."*

To help you embrace change and find deeper fulfillment in 2025, I offer a 5-step guide for embracing the new year.

Step 1: Focus on Your Spiritual Journey
This step may seem unexpected, but focusing on your spiritual self-first is essential. We are made of spirit, soul, mind and body—each part essential to the whole. While we often prioritize our mental or physical health, nurturing your spiritual self is just as important.

Connecting with something greater—whether God, the universe, or a higher power—it transforms your mindset, attitude, and actions. For me, this means prayer, reflection, and connecting with a like-minded community. A strong spiritual foundation brings lasting peace and joy.

Step 2: Embody and Inspire Hope
Hope is essential for personal and collective growth. It's about believing in renewal—not just in the world but also within your own life. Take time to reflect on areas where you need hope—whether in relationships, work, or personal growth—and let that hope inspire positive action.

Look for ways to inspire hope in others. Small acts of kindness can ignite hope in someone else's life.

Step 3: Live Out Peace with Others
Peace is not just about the quiet within; it's also about how we interact with others. Consider what's currently stealing your peace. To foster well-being, let go of stress, forgive others, and seek moments of stillness to reconnect with your inner calm. When you embody peace, you naturally spread it to those around you.

Step 4: Spread Joy Wherever You Go
This New Year, embrace joy and excitement for the good things ahead. Ask yourself every day: *"How can I practice joy and commit to spreading it today?"* Even small actions can create ripples of happiness in your life and in the lives of others.

Step 5: Be Love
The final step is love. Reflect on how you can express love throughout 2025—not just through grand gestures but through everyday acts of kindness. Love has the power to heal, connect, and transform lives, both for others and for yourself. Take one small action each day that reflects love. Whether through a kind word, a listening ear, or engaging in mindful relaxation, love is something you can be and share every day.

Conclusion: Live Your Values in 2025
I invite you to live out hope, peace, joy, and love this year. Let these values guide you through 2025, making each day meaningful and connected.

"This New Year, may you find peace in the stillness, hope in the darkness, love in every moment, and joy in every encounter."

CONNECT WITH PAULA
www.instagram.com/beyondtofreedom
www.facebook.com/beyondtofreedom
www.linkedin.com/in/paulalamb
www.linktr.ee/podcasterpaula

BREATHWORK FOR PEACEFUL LIVING

by J Cangialosi, LCPC, Therapist at Relief Mental Health

Life can tend to be hectic, busy and overwhelming. Achieving a state of calm and peacefulness can seem like an uphill battle. However, one oftentimes overlooked tool can play a crucial role in accessing this. Breathwork. Breathwork is a conscious, intentional practice of controlling the breath for the purpose of fostering emotional balance, reducing stress and anxiety, and improving overall wellbeing.

How Does it Work
Breathwork is rooted in the mind-body connection. Physically, this type of breathing assists the autonomic nervous system which is what regulates the heart rate and stress responses. By using breathwork to control the breathing, individuals are able to shift from a state of *"fight-or-flight"* to a resting state, lowering the stress hormone cortisol.

Breathwork Practices
There are several types of breathwork to engage in that will bring about calm and peace. Below are some commonly used strategies:

Diaphragmatic or Belly Breathing
This method is purposefully taking deep breaths that enter the diaphragm or abdomen. Correct practice will cause the belly to swell instead of the chest to rise. This has a significant impact on lowering tension and anxiety, despite how simple it is.

How to Practice: Place one hand on your belly and the other hand on your chest. Take a slow, deep inhale through your nose ensuring that the breath goes beyond your chest and into your belly. Look for the hand on your belly to rise. Then, slowly release the air through your mouth.

Benefits: Belly breathing will activate the parasympathetic nervous system which will lower heart rate and promote calm.

Box Breathing
Another popular breathwork technique is box breathing. Due to its structure and ease of practice, this method is frequently used. In box breathing, breaths are inhaled, held, and exhaled in equal numbers to form a box.

How to Practice: To begin, take a four-count breath through your nose and hold it for another four counts. After that, hold for another four counts before exhaling for a final four counts.

Benefits: By regulating the body's levels of carbon dioxide and oxygen, box breathing improves concentration.

Alternate Nostril
This form of breathwork originates from yoga practices as it is believed that it balances the body's energy.

How to Practice: Using your forefinger and thumb, close your right nostril with your thumb and inhale slowly through your left nostril. Hold the breath while you release your thumb, opening your right nostril. With breath held, close your left nostril using your forefinger and then slowly release your breath through your now open right nostril. Repeat this cycle several times, alternating nostrils.

Benefits: This strategy works to slow breathing down which can prove particularly helpful if anxiety becomes heightened as it helps to slow the breathing. Alternate nostril breathing supports focus and attention span.

4-7-8 Breathing
This technique is to promote relaxation and to assist with sleep quality. The important factor here is that the exhale is double the length of the inhale.

How to Practice: Inhale through your nose for a count of four, hold the breath for a count of 7 and then slowly exhale through your mouth for a full count of eight. Benefits: The longer exhale than inhale also stimulates the vagus nerve, promoting relaxation.

Mental Health Benefits of Breathwork
Breathwork provides several benefits and positive effects on mental health which have been supported by clinical evidence and scientific research.
- **Stress Reduction**: Controlled breathing lowers cortisol levels, reduces heart rate and loosens tight muscles, all of which create a sense of calm. The techniques as described above are especially effective to reduce anxiety in the moment.
- **Emotional Regulation**: As a tool in enhancing relaxation, breathwork also improves the ability to manage emotions more effectively. Deep breathing helps to balance the emotions, assisting in the ability to process through them.
- **Improved Sleep**: Can't sleep? Try some breathwork. At bedtime, lay comfortably in bed, close your eyes and begin your preferred breathwork technique. This will help to slow the breathing, quite the mind and prepare the body for sleep. Breathwork is very commonly used as a strategy for treating insomnia.

How to Make it Happen
In order to most effectively realize all of these benefits, breathing exercises really should be utilized on a consistent, daily basis. The good news is that it does not require extensive amounts of time to practice.

As with any new habit formation, start small. Begin with a few minutes of breathwork upon waking up or at bedtime, gradually increasing the number of minutes in practice. It helps to pair this new habit with other activities as this will establish a routine. You may also opt to utilize an app or a video of guided meditation and breathing exercises to help you get started.

Breathwork is an amazing tool that supports overall wellbeing in physical body and mental health by offering greater peace, calm and resilience. Whether it be to improve quality of sleep, reduce stress, or balance nerves, breathwork offers easy access to a natural and effective tool.

CONNECT WITH J

www.reliefmh.com
www.reliefmh.com/what-we-treat/anxiety
www.facebook.com/reliefmentalhealth
www.instagram.com/reliefmentalhealth
www.tiktok.com/@reliefmentalhealth
www.linkedin.com/company/relief-mh
www.x.com/reliefmh

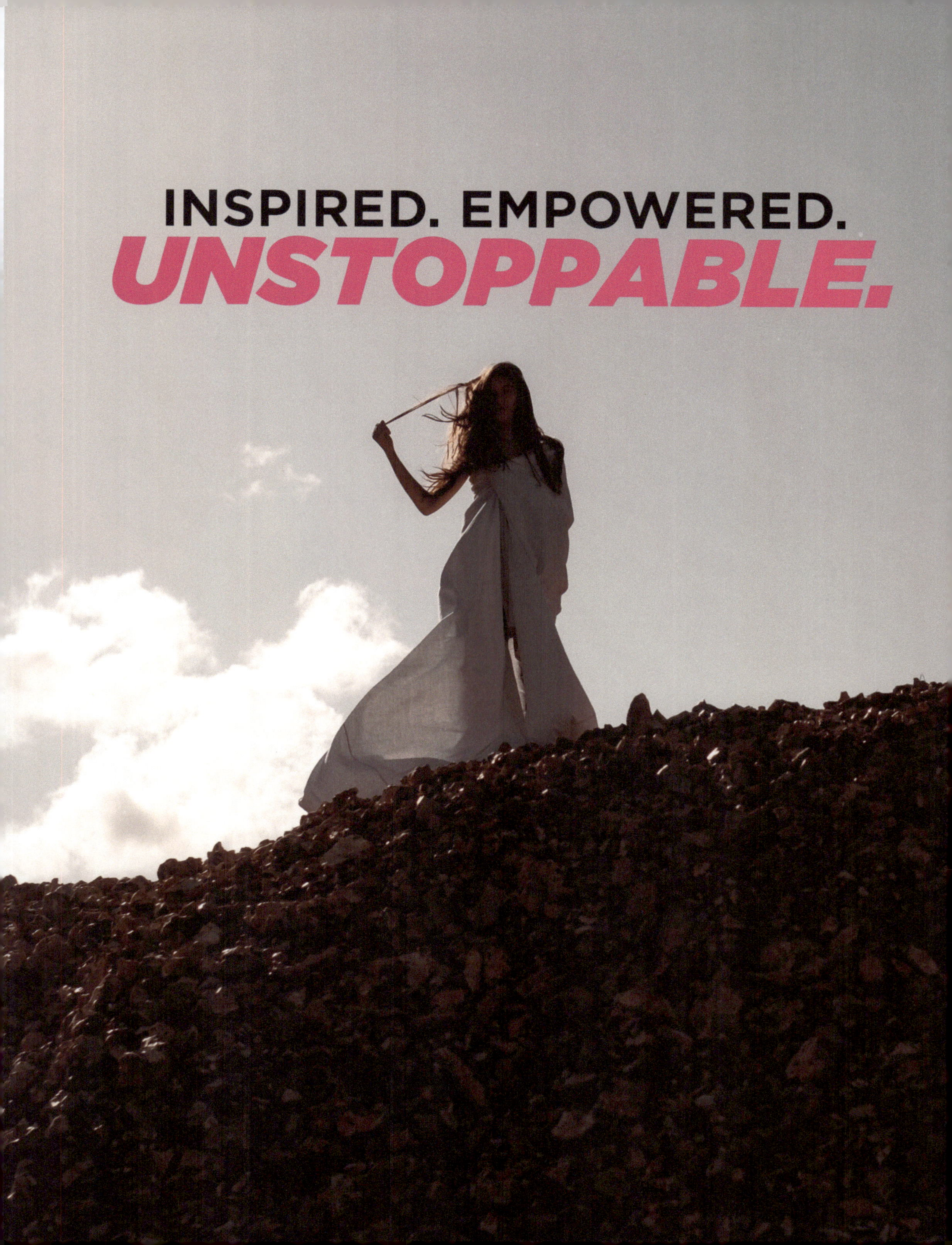
INSPIRED. EMPOWERED.
UNSTOPPABLE.

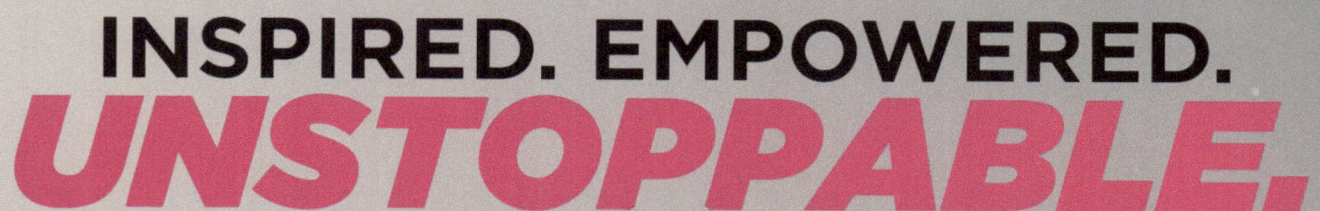

BUILDING RESILIENT RELATIONSHIPS: HOW SOCIAL CONNECTIONS CONTRIBUTE TO EMOTIONAL AND PHYSICAL WELLNESS

Amidst the challenges and stressors of modern life, one of the most powerful resources for emotional and physical wellness lies in the strength of our social connections. Our social networks—whether they consist of family, friends, colleagues, or community members—are essential in shaping both our emotional and physical health. From establishing emotional resilience to improving overall wellness, the quality of our connections significantly influences how we feel, how we cope with challenges, and how we experience joy.

The Science Behind Social Connection
Humans are naturally wired for connection. This innate need for social interaction is supported by extensive research, which consistently demonstrates how our relationships influence our mental and physical health. Those with strong social ties are more likely to experience longer lifespans, lower risks of chronic illness, and better mental health outcomes.

Social engagement activates the release of oxytocin, the *"feel-good"* hormone that creates feelings of trust and affection. Oxytocin is not only essential for creating bonds with others, but it also helps reduce stress and anxiety, enabling us to better navigate difficult situations. Furthermore, research has shown that social connections contribute to lower blood pressure, enhanced immune function, and an overall sense of happiness and well-being.

The Power of Emotional Support
Perhaps one of the greatest gifts of resilient relationships is the emotional support they provide. Life's challenges—whether personal or professional—are inevitable, but having a solid support system to rely on can help us manage stress and adversity more effectively. This emotional safety net comes in many forms: from a comforting hug from a loved one to a heart-to-heart conversation with a close friend.

Emotional support plays a critical role in buffering the negative effects of stress and trauma. Studies show that individuals who have robust social support networks are less likely to suffer from anxiety or depression, even during difficult times.

The sense of belonging we derive from our relationships enhances our emotional stability, fortifying us against the ups and downs of life.

Social Ties and Physical Health
While the emotional benefits of social connections are widely recognized, their impact on physical health is equally significant. Research shows that individuals with close, supportive relationships tend to experience better heart health, lower cholesterol levels, and stronger immune systems. This is largely due to the stress-relieving benefits of social bonds, as chronic stress is known to contribute to many serious health conditions.

In addition, social connections encourage healthier lifestyle choices. Having friends or family to share activities with—such as going to the gym, preparing nutritious meals, or participating in outdoor activities—can make it easier to stick to health goals. The accountability and motivation that come from socializing with others can lead to positive changes in exercise habits and dietary choices.

Simply put, the act of socializing itself can yield physical benefits. Engaging in shared activities, whether it's a walk in the park, a workout session, or a cooking class, brings people together in ways that support physical health and contribute to overall vitality.

Building and Nurturing Social Connections
So, how do we cultivate and maintain these meaningful relationships? The first step is recognizing the value of connection and actively making time for it. Whether it's scheduling regular coffee dates with friends or joining community groups that share your interests, the effort you put into building relationships pays off in both emotional and physical health benefits.

Being present and actively listening in your interactions is key. It's important to engage with empathy and authenticity, which strengthens the bond and ensures the relationship is mutually supportive. Don't forget that social connections are a two-way street—showing up for others is just as important as having others show up for you.

True wellness is not just about eating healthy or exercising regularly; it also involves establishing deep, meaningful relationships that contribute to our emotional and physical vitality. In a world that often feels isolating, the resilience of our social connections can help us thrive in every aspect of life. By prioritizing and nurturing these relationships, we can unlock greater joy, reduce stress, and experience a sense of fulfillment that goes beyond physical health. As we continue our journey toward holistic well-being, let's remember that the connections we cultivate are just as important as the self-care routines we follow.

CONNECT WITH US
www.sherisesstudios.com

HOW I UNEARTHED MY DHARMA AND BECAME AN ACCIDENTAL AYURVEDA DIGESTIVE HEALTH COACH

by Amayra Morales

Ever since I was a little girl, I've had an insatiable urge to help. Whether it was bringing home injured animals, assisting elderly people across the street, or lending a hand wherever I could, helping others became second nature. By my mid-20s, traveling and volunteering had become the highlights of my adventures. In 2012, I landed a dream job in Laos with an Australian NGO, fulfilling that deep-seated desire. But when my year-long contract ended, I found myself at a crossroads. The fire to help was still burning, but I felt lost on how to channel it.

So, I did what many do when faced with uncertainty—I entered the corporate world as I needed to make ends meet. What I thought would be a temporary detour stretched into a decade. Before I knew it, ten years had flown by, and I found myself hitting rock bottom. One day, I ended up in the hospital, completely burnt out.

I strongly believe that my burnout wasn't due to my stressful job but rather because I was doing something that didn't light me up.

There's nothing quite like staring at the sterile ceiling of a hospital room and asking yourself, *"How did I get here?"* I had heard of people hitting rock bottom, but I never thought it would happen to me. Yet, there I was, grappling with the realisation that this wasn't a sudden fall —it was a slow, steady accumulation of ignoring all the signs my body had been sending for years.

As strange as it sounds, I'm grateful for that wake-up call from the universe. When I walked out of the hospital, I knew one thing for certain: my time in the corporate world was over.

Within a month, I booked a one-way flight to Bangalore, India, to pursue a dream I had long put on the back burner—Yoga Teacher Training. But not long after I arrived, I got sick again. This time, though, it felt different. I was in a foreign country with no choice but to trust the process and believe I would get better.

Through a series of fortunate events, I found myself in an Ayurveda clinic. That was the turning point. I finally discovered the healing modality that would help me regain my health.

After completing my treatment at the clinic, I felt incredible—a sign that I needed to dive deeper into this ancient wisdom. So, I pursued and completed my Master Ayurvedic Digestion and Nutrition certification.

But even then, I wasn't entirely sure what my next step would be. I began sharing what I had learned during my studies, and soon enough, people started reaching out for advice. Then, my cousin said something that changed everything: *"Why don't you turn this into a business and get paid for what you're already doing?"*

Me, an entrepreneur?

The thought had never crossed my mind, but it made perfect sense. I was truly enjoying helping people improve their health.

And that's how my entrepreneurial journey began. I became an accidental Ayurveda digestive health coach, transforming my passion for healing into a purposeful career.

I now realize that my health challenges were a gift because they forced me to overcome obstacles in order to help others facing similar struggles. My Ayurvedic doctor taught me that health isn't the end goal but rather a vehicle to live your Dharma - your purpose. When you're consumed by health issues, you can lose sight of the bigger picture— that we've all come here to live your best life.

How we do it is through our own unique magic sauce. Now t's time to reconnect with your Dharma.

CONNECT WITH AMAYRA

www.amayramorales.com
www.facebook.com/amayra.r.morales
www.instagram.com/amayra.morales

FITNESS FOR THE SOUL:
FUN AND ENERGIZING WORKOUTS THAT SPARK JOY

With so many responsibilities pulling us in different directions, fitness can seem like just another duty on the to-do list. However, what if your exercise routine could become a source of joy and inner fulfillment, nourishing your body, mind, and soul?

1. Dance Your Way to Joy

Dance is a dynamic blend of movement and expression that uplifts the spirit and invigorates the body. Whether it's salsa, hip-hop, or ballet, dancing allows you to let loose, release tension, and enjoy the rhythm of your favorite tunes. You don't need professional skills—just a willingness to move and embrace the joy of music. Dance can boost your mood, improve coordination, and help you feel deeply connected to your body. Whether you take a class or dance solo at home, the experience is a liberating way to combine fitness with fun.

2. Yoga: The Perfect Harmony of Body and Soul

Yoga is a transformative practice that combines mindful breathing, gentle stretching, and purposeful movement to nurture the body and calm the mind. Offering a wide variety of styles, from restorative yoga to intense vinyasa flows, it accommodates every fitness level and mood. This ancient practice helps relieve stress, enhance flexibility, and build strength while fostering a sense of inner peace and balance. By focusing on being present in each pose, yoga allows you to reconnect with your soul and find joy in the art of stillness and movement alike.

3. Walking in Nature: Grounding Your Energy

Immersing yourself in nature through walking is a simple yet profoundly rejuvenating experience. A stroll through a park, a hike in the woods, or a walk along the beach not only clears the mind but also revitalizes the spirit. Surrounded by fresh air and natural beauty, you can reduce stress, improve mood, and boost your physical health with this low-impact exercise. Walking in nature offers a mindful escape from daily pressures, grounding your energy and enhancing your overall well-being.

4. Strength Training with a Twist

Strength training becomes soul-nourishing when approached with a focus on empowerment and fun. Instead of fixating on numbers, embrace the thrill of building resilience and power. By incorporating dynamic movements like kettlebell swings, battle ropes, or playful partner exercises, you can transform a traditional workout into an engaging adventure. These activities stimulate your muscles, energize your mind, and keep your routine fresh and exciting. Strength training not only tones your body but also builds confidence and a sense of accomplishment.

5. Tai Chi: A Moving Meditation

Tai Chi is a gentle martial art that fuses slow, controlled movements with mindful breathing. Often called *"meditation in motion,"* this practice fosters balance, mental clarity, and inner peace. Ideal for all ages, Tai Chi helps enhance flexibility, reduce stress, and promote relaxation without high physical intensity. As you move gracefully through its sequences, you cultivate a harmonious connection between your mind and body, making Tai Chi an excellent way to nourish your soul while staying active.

6. Rebounding: Jump for Joy

Rebounding on a mini-trampoline is an exhilarating, low-impact workout that sparks joy and boosts cardiovascular health. The playful act of bouncing not only tones your legs and core but also releases endorphins, the brain's *"feel-good"* chemicals. This fun activity can be done at home, making it a convenient way to energize your day. Whether you're aiming for a quick cardio session or simply enjoying the thrill of jumping, rebounding leaves you feeling lighter, happier, and more alive.

7. Martial Arts: Empower Your Mind and Body

Martial arts, such as kickboxing or karate, combine intense physical activity with mental discipline and self-confidence. These practices challenge your body while enhancing focus and resilience. Learning new techniques and mastering movements instills a sense of empowerment and accomplishment. Beyond fitness, martial arts cultivate inner strength, reduce stress, and help you channel energy constructively. Whether training solo or in a group, martial arts promote a holistic sense of well-being.

Incorporating Fun and Energizing Workouts into Your Life

Fitness for the soul lies in choosing activities that resonate deeply with you. When exercise is enjoyable, it transforms into a celebration of vitality and inner peace rather than a chore. By embracing workouts that bring joy, you can nurture your body, mind, and spirit, creating a holistic approach to wellness that enhances every aspect of your life.

CONNECT WITH US

www.sherisesstudios.com

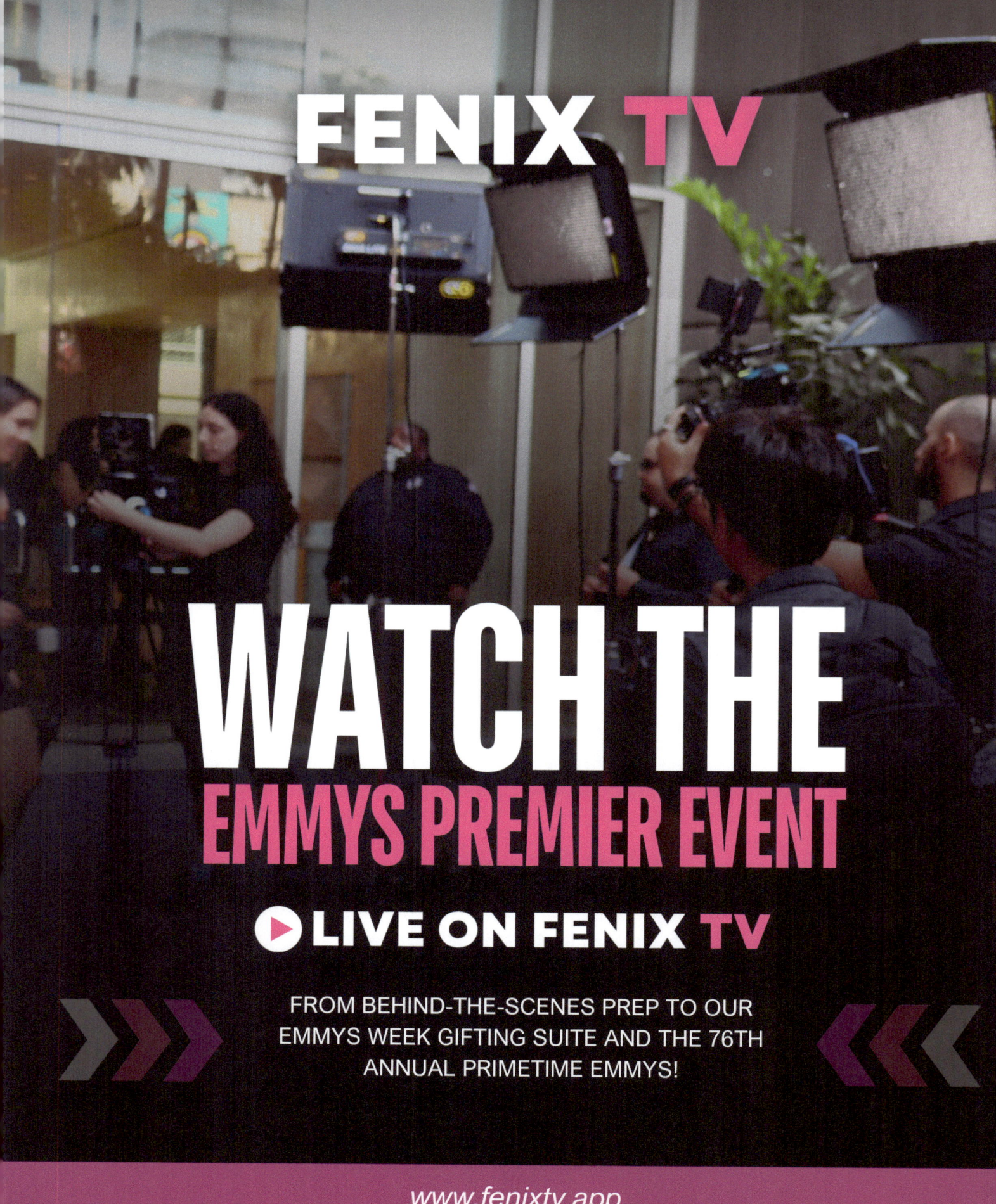

WOMAN IN MOTION: FULL BODY ENRICHMENT THROUGH SACRED DANCE

by Karyne Daniels

Every woman holds a sacred rhythm within, waiting to be set free. In our fast-paced world, where demands often overshadow self-care, it's vital to reconnect with this inner dance. As a sacred dance specialist, I've witnessed its transformative power and am here to help you unlock this gift and experience profound healing.

MOVEMENT IS LIFE

From our first breath, we are in motion. Life is a dance, a series of movements that express our choices, deepest emotions, and dreams. Yet, many women feel disconnected from their bodies, burdened by the weight of responsibilities, and unsure how to reclaim their natural rhythm. The truth is, you don't need to be a trained dancer to experience the benefits of movement. Sacred dance is accessible to all, regardless of age, background, or fitness level.

DISCOVERING SACRED DANCE

Sacred dance is merely movement that brings focus to God, uniting mind, body, and spirit in a harmonious flow. My journey with sacred dance began at a young age, influenced by both Polynesian and urban contemporary dance. I've developed a unique movement system that integrates Soul-Body-Spirit enrichment with prayer and meditation to foster deep healing and embodiment - an invitation to every woman to embrace her true essence and awaken her inner divine dancer.

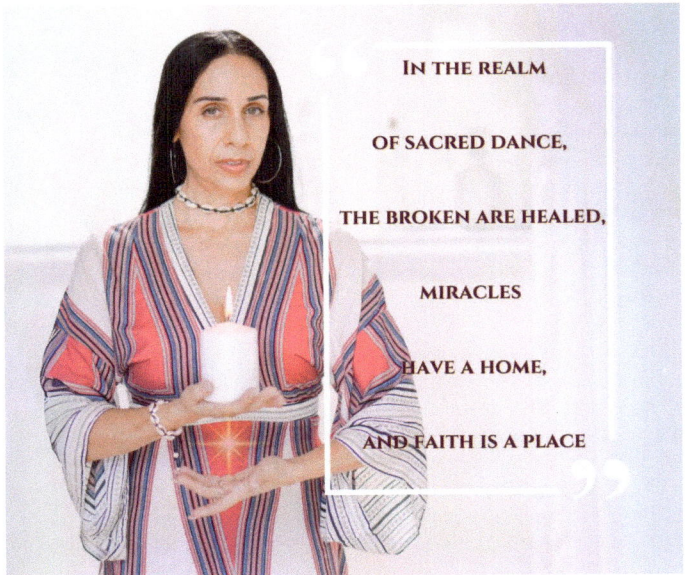

IN THE REALM

OF SACRED DANCE,

THE BROKEN ARE HEALED,

MIRACLES

HAVE A HOME,

AND FAITH IS A PLACE

BENEFITS OF SACRED DANCE

Emotional Healing: Sacred dance allows us to release emotions and traumas, offering a safe space for deep healing. As we move, we release what no longer serves us, inviting in joy and peace.

Physical Wellness: Sacred dance supports embodiment, mental clarity, and blood flow. It moves energy through the body, bringing a sense of aliveness. It is a movement & devotion that turns on the heart-light.

Spiritual Connection: Through sacred dance, we connect with the Divine, experiencing a profound sense of oneness. It is prayer in motion.

A DANCE DIRECTIVE

To begin your dance journey, create a sacred space in your home. This could be a corner of a room where you feel free to express yourself. Light a candle, and take a few moments to center yourself. Here's a simple dance directive to get you started:

Song Suggestion: *"Morning Prayer"* by Olivia Foa'i

Opening Prayer Sample:

"Oh, Father Creator, dance with me, and receive the prayers I offer to you through my spirit-led movement. I long to feel you, hear you, see you, and sense your Spirit with me now...In Jesus' name, amen."

Start Music:

Grounding: Stand with your feet hip-width apart, knees slightly bent. Close your eyes and take a few deep breaths, feeling the connection between your feet and the earth.

Flowing Movements: Begin gently swaying, moving from side to side, with hands lifted to heaven. Let your body respond to the music.

Heart Opening: Place your hands over your heart, feeling its rhythm. With each beat, imagine your heart expanding with love and gratitude. Slowly extend your arms outward, letting go of the old while receiving the new.

Expressing Joy: Smile on purpose. Allow yourself to move freely. Let the joy within you burst forth, celebrating the freedom to move and express your soul.

Closing: Gradually bring your movements to a close, returning to gentle sways. Place your hands in prayer position at your heart, offering gratitude, and a closing prayer.

Every woman has a dance within her, a sacred expression waiting to be celebrated. By saying yes to sacred dance, you invite a new template into your life. Whether you dance in the privacy of your home or join a community, know that you are part of a beautiful tradition of women in motion. Your next miracle could be one dance away!

CONNECT WITH KARYNE

www.sacreddancepath.org
www.facebook.com/karyne.daniels
www.instagram.com/sacred_dance_path

HEART HEALTH AWARENESS: TIPS FOR CARDIOVASCULAR HEALTH IN HONOR OF AMERICAN HEART MONTH

In a world where the fast pace of life often overshadows the importance of well-being, American Heart Month serves as a vital reminder to pause and focus on cardiovascular health. Your heart beats tirelessly over 100,000 times a day, making it one of the most crucial organs to nurture. Heart health is not just a concern for those with pre-existing conditions—it's a universal priority that affects people of all ages and lifestyles. This February, embrace actionable strategies to boost your heart health and lead a life of resilience and vitality. Whether you're starting fresh or refining your wellness habits, these tips will help you make choices that protect and empower your heart.

1. Prioritize a Heart-Healthy Diet

The food you consume has a profound impact on your heart. A heart-healthy diet emphasizes fresh, nutrient-rich options such as fruits, vegetables, whole grains, lean proteins, and healthy fats. Adding foods like leafy greens, berries, salmon, walnuts, and flaxseeds can lower cholesterol, reduce inflammation, and support cardiovascular function. At the same time, cutting back on processed snacks, sugary beverages, and trans fats is essential to minimizing risk factors for heart disease. By focusing on whole, unprocessed foods, you create a dietary foundation that supports heart health and overall well-being.

2. Stay Physically Active

Regular exercise is a cornerstone of cardiovascular health, strengthening the heart muscle, improving circulation, and aiding in weight management. Experts recommend at least 150 minutes of moderate aerobic activity per week, such as brisk walking, cycling, or swimming. To enhance the benefits, incorporate strength training exercises like resistance bands or weightlifting to tone muscles and support the heart. Choose activities you genuinely enjoy, whether it's dancing, hiking, or yoga, to ensure consistency and make physical activity an integral, enjoyable part of your routine.

3. Manage Stress Effectively

Stress, particularly when chronic, is a significant contributor to heart disease. It raises blood pressure, causes inflammation, and can lead to unhealthy coping behaviors like overeating or smoking.

Incorporating mindfulness techniques such as meditation, deep breathing, or yoga can help calm your mind and reduce stress hormones. Maintaining strong social connections is equally important—sharing time with loved ones offers emotional support and alleviates feelings of isolation. Set aside daily *"me time"* for activities you love, like reading or painting, to further counterbalance stress.

4. Keep Your Blood Pressure and Cholesterol in Check

High blood pressure and cholesterol are often silent threats, causing damage before noticeable symptoms appear. Regular monitoring is crucial for staying ahead of potential issues. Simple lifestyle adjustments, such as reducing salt intake, increasing dietary fiber, and quitting smoking, can significantly lower these numbers. Additionally, adhering to your doctor's advice, including prescribed medications, is key to managing and improving your cardiovascular health. Being proactive about your heart's well-being ensures you remain in control of your health.

5. Prioritize Sleep

Quality sleep is vital for heart health, yet it's often overlooked. Poor sleep patterns increase the risk of heart disease, diabetes, and obesity. Aim for 7-9 hours of rest each night by establishing a consistent bedtime routine. Reduce screen time at least an hour before bed, and create a serene sleep environment by keeping your bedroom cool, dark, and quiet. By prioritizing rest, you give your heart the recovery time it needs to function optimally.

6. Break Unhealthy Habits

Smoking and excessive alcohol consumption are two habits that negatively affect cardiovascular health. Quitting smoking, whether through counseling, support groups, or nicotine replacement therapies, can significantly improve your heart and lung function. Moderating alcohol intake—limiting consumption to one drink per day for women and two for men—helps avoid undue strain on your heart. Eliminating these harmful behaviors paves the way for a healthier, more robust cardiovascular system.

7. Stay Educated and Spread Awareness

Knowledge is a powerful tool in preventing heart disease. Learn to recognize warning signs of heart attack or stroke, such as chest pain, shortness of breath, or sudden numbness. Share this awareness with friends, family, and your community to promote a culture of heart health. Engage in initiatives like local heart walks or awareness campaigns during American Heart Month to inspire others to adopt healthy habits and take charge of their cardiovascular well-being.

Your Heart Deserves Care Every Day

Heart health is a lifelong commitment that extends beyond American Heart Month. By incorporating small, consistent changes into your diet, activity level, and daily habits, you not only protect your heart but also invest in a vibrant, joyful future. Let February be your starting point for a healthier lifestyle. Take care of your heart—it's the rhythm of your life.

NOURISH WITH LOVE: HEART-HEALTHY RECIPES AND NUTRITION TIPS

Your heart works tirelessly every second of every day, keeping you alive and thriving. It deserves a little extra care and attention, especially when it comes to the food you choose to nourish it. In this edition of Vitality Digest Magazine, we're diving into the delicious and healthful world of heart-friendly recipes and nutrition tips, showing you that eating for your heart can be both satisfying and simple.

The Heart of the Matter

Heart disease remains a leading cause of death worldwide, but the good news is that lifestyle changes, particularly in diet, can significantly reduce your risk. A heart-healthy diet not only lowers bad cholesterol and blood pressure but also helps maintain a healthy weight, reducing strain on your heart. By making mindful choices and focusing on nutrient-rich, natural ingredients, you can protect your cardiovascular health while enjoying every bite.

Building a Heart-Healthy Plate

A heart-smart diet is all about balance and variety. It's not about deprivation but about making thoughtful choices that support your overall well-being. Here's a guide to building a plate that loves your heart as much as you love great food:

- **Focus on Fruits and Vegetables:** These vibrant powerhouses are loaded with vitamins, minerals, and antioxidants that fight inflammation and support heart health. Aim for a variety of colors to maximize nutrient intake.
- **Embrace Whole Grains:** Quinoa, brown rice, oatmeal, and whole-grain bread provide fiber, which helps reduce cholesterol levels.
- **Choose Healthy Fats:** Not all fats are created equal. Opt for monounsaturated and polyunsaturated fats from sources like avocados, nuts, seeds, and olive oil. Avoid trans fats and limit saturated fats.
- **Lean Protein Options:** Skinless poultry, fish (especially fatty fish like salmon and mackerel), beans, and legumes are excellent sources of protein without the artery-clogging saturated fats found in red meats.
- **Limit Salt and Sugar:** Excess sodium and sugar can lead to high blood pressure and other heart issues. Season your meals with herbs, spices, and citrus for flavor without the added salt.

Heart-Healthy Recipes to Try

Here are two easy, delicious recipes designed with your heart in mind:

Berry Bliss Breakfast Bowl

Start your day with a nutrient-packed breakfast that's as beautiful as it is good for your heart.

Ingredients:
- 1 cup plain, unsweetened Greek yogurt
- ½ cup fresh or frozen mixed berries (blueberries, strawberries, raspberries)
- 2 tablespoons granola (low-sugar)
- 1 tablespoon chia seeds
- 1 teaspoon honey (optional)

Instructions:
1. Spoon the Greek yogurt into a bowl.
2. Top with berries, granola, and chia seeds.
3. Drizzle with honey if desired.

Why it's heart-healthy: Greek yogurt provides protein and calcium, berries are rich in antioxidants, and chia seeds offer heart-friendly omega-3 fatty acids.

Salmon and Quinoa Power Bowl

This hearty dish is perfect for lunch or dinner, offering a balance of lean protein, whole grains, and healthy fats.

Ingredients:
- 1 salmon fillet (about 4-6 ounces)
- ½ cup cooked quinoa
- 1 cup steamed broccoli
- ¼ avocado, sliced
- 1 tablespoon olive oil
- Juice of ½ lemon
- Salt and pepper to taste

Instructions:
1. Preheat the oven to 375°F (190°C). Season the salmon with salt, pepper, and a squeeze of lemon. Bake for 12-15 minutes or until cooked through.
2. Arrange the cooked quinoa, steamed broccoli, and avocado slices in a bowl.
3. Top with the baked salmon. Drizzle with olive oil and the remaining lemon juice.

Why it's heart-healthy: Salmon is rich in omega-3 fatty acids, quinoa provides fiber and protein, and the avocado and olive oil add healthy fats that support cardiovascular health.

Lifestyle Tips for a Healthier Heart

Eating well is a cornerstone of heart health, but pairing your diet with other lifestyle habits will amplify your efforts:

1. **Stay Active:** Aim for at least 30 minutes of moderate exercise most days of the week. Activities like walking, swimming, or cycling can strengthen your heart and improve circulation.
2. **Manage Stress:** Chronic stress can take a toll on your heart. Incorporate relaxation techniques like meditation, deep breathing, or yoga into your routine.
3. **Get Enough Sleep:** Sleep is essential for overall health. Adults should aim for 7-9 hours per night.
4. **Hydrate:** Drinking plenty of water supports blood flow and overall bodily function.
5. **Quit Smoking:** Smoking damages blood vessels and increases your risk of heart disease. If you smoke, seek support to quit.

Love Your Heart, One Bite at a Time

Taking care of your heart doesn't have to mean sacrificing flavor or enjoyment in your meals. By incorporating heart-healthy ingredients, preparing simple, delicious recipes, and making small but impactful lifestyle changes, you can nourish your body with love and set the foundation for a healthier, more vibrant life. Remember, every bite and choice you make is a step toward a stronger, happier heart. Here's to a life filled with vitality, one meal at a time.

SKULL SUGAR COSMETICS: A BOLD FUSION OF BEAUTY, WELLNESS, AND SELF-EXPRESSION

by Jamie O'Neill

Jamie O'Neill, the creative force behind *Skull Sugar Cosmetics*, has carved a unique space in the beauty industry with her bold, unconventional aesthetic. Her brand, rooted in self-expression and wellness, reflects a balance between striking visual appeal and health-conscious ingredients. Jamie's journey from a makeup artist to a holistic health practitioner and author speaks to her dedication to creating products that empower individuals both inside and out.

The Birth of Skull Sugar Cosmetics

Jamie's inspiration for *Skull Sugar Cosmetics* stemmed from her passion for makeup artistry and her desire to create a brand that set trends rather than followed them. *"Back then, there weren't many talc- and paraben-free options in the market,"* she explains. *"Ensuring my clients' safety was just as important as creating standout products."* This dual focus on aesthetics and safety defines the brand's ethos.

The brand's bold, rebellious aesthetic was influenced by Jamie's love of contrasts—light and dark, beauty and rebellion. Skull Sugar blends these elements to celebrate the beauty in being different. *"It's about making a statement while feeling good about what you're putting on your skin,"* Jamie shares.

Influences from FashioNXT

Jamie's role as the key makeup artist for *FashioNXT* deeply shaped her approach to beauty. *"Working behind the scenes taught me that makeup isn't just an accessory; it's a tool for storytelling,"* Jamie reflects. The high-pressure environment of fashion shows pushed her to experiment with colors, textures, and techniques, reinforcing the importance of quality, long-lasting products.

Her experience in the fashion world directly influenced the development of *Skull Sugar* products, which deliver professional-level performance while remaining accessible to everyday users. *"Models need to look flawless under intense lights, and that's the standard I brought to my product line,"* she says.

Photo Credit: Mark Muzzy

Photo Credit: Cardwell Photography

Recognition and Expansion

Being featured in Forbes NY and Forbes England marked a turning point for Jamie and her brand. *"The features brought visibility and credibility that helped take Skull Sugar to new heights,"* she acknowledges. Already enjoying international exposure, the recognition from Forbes further solidified the brand's standing in the industry.

The success also motivated Jamie to push her creative boundaries, leading to new product releases and innovations. *"It validated all the hard work I had put in and inspired me to evolve Skull Sugar into something even bolder,"* she says.

Holistic Approach to Beauty

Jamie's holistic health background is a crucial influence on her beauty business. As a holistic practitioner, she views wellness from a whole-person perspective—mind, body, and spirit. *"When developing products, I focus not only on aesthetics but on creating formulations that are safe, gentle, and free of harmful ingredients,"* she explains. *"My clients' health is always a top priority."*

This approach stems from her belief that true beauty comes from within. She emphasizes that makeup should enhance rather than mask a person's natural features. *"I aim to provide products that help people feel good inside and out,"* Jamie adds, aligning with a wellness-focused, holistic approach to beauty.

Spiritual Practices and Empowerment

Spirituality plays a foundational role in Jamie's life and work. *"Meditation, tarot, and connecting with my intuition are daily rituals that keep me grounded,"* she shares. These practices not only guide her as a holistic healer but also influence her work with *Skull Sugar*. *"Beauty isn't just about appearances—it's about confidence, self-love, and authenticity,"* Jamie notes.

Her spiritual journey informs her belief that makeup is a form of self-expression and empowerment. Through her products, she aims to help people connect with their true selves while encouraging them to embrace their inner light. *"I want people to feel confident in their own skin and to see makeup as an extension of their unique identity,"* she says.

Writing *"Journey of My Soul"*

Jamie's personal journey of self-discovery, marked by overcoming addiction, trauma, and abuse, inspired her to write *Journey of My Soul*. *"The book was born out of a deep calling to share my story and help others who are struggling,"* she reveals. Jamie's raw and honest account of her battle with addiction to alcohol and cocaine, as well as the trauma of abuse, serves as a guide for those seeking healing.

"I wanted Journey of My Soul to be a light for those who need it, showing that transformation is possible even in our darkest moments," Jamie says. By sharing her story, she hopes to inspire others to find their own path to self-discovery and healing.

Tarot Readings as a Tool for Growth

As a tarot reader, Jamie uses the cards to guide her clients on their personal journeys. *"I see tarot as a powerful tool for self-reflection, not fortune-telling,"* she explains. Her readings help clients uncover hidden truths and patterns, offering clarity and guidance. *"Each reading is tailored to where the client is on their path, whether they're seeking healing or direction,"* she adds.

Jamie's broader mission is to help people embrace their true selves, and tarot readings are one of the ways she does this. *"I encourage clients to trust their intuition, let go of self-doubt, and step fully into their authenticity,"* she says.

Balancing Multiple Passions

Balancing her roles as a beauty entrepreneur, holistic practitioner, and author has not been without challenges. *"One of the biggest challenges was time management,"* Jamie admits. *"There were times when it felt like I was being pulled in multiple directions at once."*

However, Jamie learned to embrace integration rather than compartmentalization. *"Instead of seeing these as separate aspects of my life, I began to view them as complementary pieces of a larger puzzle,"* she says. Her overarching mission of helping people feel empowered guided her through the challenges.

Learning to delegate tasks and prioritize self-care also played a crucial role in maintaining balance. *"Practicing self-care and setting healthy boundaries helped me stay grounded and aligned with my purpose,"* she notes.

Advocating for Inner Healing

In an industry focused on outward appearance, Jamie advocates for inner healing and wellness. *"True beauty radiates from within, and while makeup can enhance our features, it's only part of the equation,"* she

explains. Her holistic health practice focuses on helping clients find balance in mind, body, and spirit, addressing root causes rather than superficial symptoms.

By integrating wellness into her beauty business, Jamie emphasizes the connection between health and beauty. *"I want my clients to feel good about what they're putting on their skin and to see beauty as an extension of their wellness journey,"* she says. Through this approach, Jamie helps people embrace a more holistic view of self-care, one that honors their whole being.

In the world of beauty and wellness, Jamie O'Neill's *Skull Sugar Cosmetics* stands out as a bold, empowering brand that reflects her passion for self-expression, health, and spiritual well-being. By integrating these elements into her products and practices, she offers clients a unique approach to beauty—one that celebrates inner and outer transformation alike.

JOURNEY OF MY SOUL

A guided journal by Jamie O'Neill

"The journey of our soul is the eternal expedition of self discovery, an odyssey through the cosmos of experience, where every twist & turn unveils the profound tapestry of our existence"

May this help guide you to the uncovering of your souls mission & light the way to your destination.

CONNECT WITH JAMIE

www.silvermoonoracle.com
www.linkedin.com/in/jamieloneill
www.skullsugarcosmetics.com
www.instagram.com/skullsugarcosmetics
www.amazon.com/Journey-My-Soul-Guided-Journal/dp/B0CJD8B9LC

GET A COPY TODAY!

Discover a celebration of courage and resilience in Her Unseen Battle. This inspiring book shines a light on the silent struggles women face and the strength it takes to overcome them. Through raw, unfiltered stories, women from diverse walks of life share their journeys—navigating loss, breaking free from self-doubt, challenging societal norms, and battling invisible struggles like mental health.

Each story is accompanied by practical tips, empowering affirmations, and actionable steps to help you build resilience, find healing, and reclaim your power.

With tools like mindfulness exercises, self-care strategies, and affirmations for self-love, this book offers guidance to support your own path to transformation.

Her Unseen Battle reminds us all that no struggle is too small or unseen to matter. It's a testament to the strength of the human spirit and an invitation to embrace your vulnerabilities, rise above challenges, and step into your true potential.

Your battle is seen. Your pain is valid. And within you lies the power to heal and thrive.

MENTAL FITNESS MATTERS: HOW SMALL HABITS CAN BOOST YOUR EMOTIONAL WELL-BEING

In a world that often feels fast-paced and overwhelming, prioritizing mental fitness is more important than ever. Just as physical fitness strengthens our bodies, mental fitness fortifies our emotional and psychological resilience. The good news? You don't need to overhaul your entire life to make a significant impact. Simple, consistent habits can go a long way in boosting your emotional well-being and helping you thrive, no matter what life throws your way.

Understanding Mental Fitness

Mental fitness refers to your ability to manage stress, maintain a positive outlook, and navigate life's challenges with clarity and balance. It's not about eliminating negative emotions or stress entirely—that's unrealistic. Instead, mental fitness is about cultivating the strength to face those moments and recover more effectively. Think of it as training your mind to be flexible, adaptive, and strong, much like how you would train a muscle at the gym.

The Power of Small Habits

When it comes to building mental fitness, small, intentional habits can create lasting change. These habits don't require hours of effort or significant financial investment. They're simple, actionable steps that integrate seamlessly into your daily routine. And over time, these small actions build momentum, contributing to a more balanced and emotionally resilient version of yourself. Let's explore a few small yet powerful habits that can transform your mental well-being:

1. Practice Gratitude Daily

Taking a moment to reflect on what you're grateful for can shift your perspective and increase your emotional resilience. Start or end your day by jotting down three things you're thankful for. They don't have to be monumental—it could be as simple as a beautiful sunrise, a kind word from a friend, or a cup of your favorite tea. Research shows that practicing gratitude can reduce stress, enhance happiness, and even improve relationships. Over time, it trains your mind to focus on the positives in life, even during challenging times.

2. Embrace Mindfulness

Mindfulness is the art of being fully present in the moment, without judgment. It can be as simple as focusing on your breath for a few minutes or savoring the taste of your food without distractions. By practicing mindfulness, you create a mental space where you can observe your thoughts and feelings without being overwhelmed by them. This not only reduces stress but also enhances your ability to respond to situations calmly and thoughtfully.

3. Prioritize Sleep

Sleep is the foundation of both physical and mental health, yet it's often the first thing we sacrifice when life gets busy. Poor sleep can amplify feelings of stress, anxiety, and irritability, making it harder to maintain emotional balance. Establish a bedtime routine that promotes restful sleep. This could include reducing screen time an hour before bed, practicing relaxation techniques like deep breathing, and creating a comfortable sleep environment. Prioritizing quality sleep can significantly improve your mood, focus, and overall mental fitness.

4. Move Your Body Regularly

Exercise isn't just for physical health—it's a powerful tool for emotional well-being too. Physical activity releases endorphins, the body's natural mood boosters, and reduces levels of stress hormones like cortisol. You don't have to commit to intense workouts to reap the benefits. Even a 15-minute walk in nature or a short yoga session can make a big difference. Find an activity you enjoy and make it a regular part of your routine.

5. Connect with Others

Human connection is vital for emotional well-being. Whether it's a heartfelt conversation with a friend, joining a supportive community, or spending quality time with family, nurturing relationships can help you feel grounded and supported. If you're feeling isolated, consider reaching out to someone you trust or exploring new social opportunities. A strong support system provides emotional strength during tough times and enhances feelings of belonging.

6. Set Boundaries

Learning to say *"no"* when necessary and setting clear boundaries is crucial for protecting your emotional energy. Overcommitting or neglecting your own needs can lead to burnout and resentment. Evaluate your commitments and prioritize what truly matters. Remember, it's okay to put your well-being first—it's not selfish; it's necessary.

Building a Resilient Mindset

Incorporating these small habits into your daily life may feel challenging at first, but consistency is key. The goal is progress, not perfection. Even small steps can lead to significant improvements in your mental fitness over time. Additionally, be patient with yourself. Building a resilient mindset is a journey, not a destination. Celebrate your efforts, no matter how small, and recognize that setbacks are a natural part of growth. Mental fitness matters because it empowers you to face life with strength, resilience, and optimism. By embracing small habits like gratitude, mindfulness, and connection, you can create a foundation for lasting emotional well-being. Remember, it's never too late to invest in your mental fitness. Start with one small habit today and watch how it transforms your life over time. With each step, you're not only improving your own well-being but also inspiring those around you to prioritize theirs. After all, a healthier, happier mind is the key to a thriving life.

CONNECT WITH US

www.sherisesstudios.com

MINDSET.

SELF-CARE RITUALS: WAYS TO NURTURE PHYSICAL AND MENTAL WELL-BEING

The hustle and bustle of everyday life can make us feel burdened by continuous responsibilities at work and home, leaving us physically and mentally drained. These pressures often create a disconnect between our well-being and the lives we lead. This is where self-care becomes essential—a practice not just about indulgence but a necessity to maintain health and balance. Self-care rituals, when embraced regularly, offer a chance to reconnect with ourselves, replenish energy, and regain equilibrium. They remind us to slow down, prioritize health, and address our emotional needs. However, self-care is not one-size-fits-all. It's about creating a personalized routine that nurtures your unique needs and sustains your well-being.

The Power of Morning Routines
A purposeful morning routine establishes the tone for the day ahead and is an essential self-care ritual. Starting your morning by checking in with yourself before facing the world helps cultivate a sense of control and calmness. This doesn't require elaborate practices; simple acts like sipping a warm cup of tea, practicing deep breathing, or stretching can energize your mind and body. Mindfulness, in particular, is a powerful addition to your mornings. Spend a few minutes meditating, journaling, or setting intentions to clear mental clutter and focus on positivity. These moments of self-nourishment ground you and prepare you to tackle the day with resilience and clarity.

Nourish Your Body with Wholesome Foods
What you feed your body profoundly impacts your energy, immune system, and mood, making nutrition a cornerstone of self-care. Incorporating fresh fruits, vegetables, lean proteins, and healthy fats into your diet supports long-term health. Beyond what you eat, how you eat matters too. Taking the time to savor meals without distractions cultivates mindfulness, enhancing your connection to food and its benefits. Preparing colorful, nutrient-dense dishes like vibrant salads or hearty vegetable soups can become a soothing ritual that nurtures both your body and spirit, turning everyday nourishment into an act of self-care.

The Healing Power of Movement
Physical activity is a self-care ritual that revitalizes both the body and mind. Exercise doesn't need to involve intense workouts; even simple movements like yoga, dancing, or walking can uplift your mood and reduce stress. These activities release endorphins, which act as natural stress relievers, while also enhancing circulation, flexibility, and sleep quality. Yoga is particularly effective, combining deliberate movements and deep breathing to strengthen your body and calm your mind. Finding joy in movement is key; when exercise feels enjoyable, it becomes a sustainable habit that enhances your overall well-being.

Restorative Sleep: The Ultimate Act of Self-Care
Sleep is the foundation of physical and mental health, making it one of the most critical self-care practices. Quality rest allows your body to repair, recharge, and restore. Creating a soothing bedtime ritual signals to your body that it's time to relax, promoting better sleep.

Dim the lights, stretch gently, or practice deep breathing before bed. Avoid screen time and opt for calming teas like chamomile or lavender to wind down. Prioritizing sleep helps combat stress, boosts immunity, and ensures you wake up feeling refreshed, ready to embrace the day ahead with vitality.

Digital Detox for Mental Clarity
In our hyper-connected world, the constant influx of notifications and information can overwhelm the mind. A daily digital detox is a self-care ritual that provides mental clarity and peace. Setting aside time to disconnect from technology allows you to reconnect with yourself and the present moment. Whether it's reading, journaling, or enjoying nature, these unplugged moments help declutter your mind and reduce stress. By creating boundaries around technology use, you regain control over your time, fostering a sense of calm and focus that benefits your overall well-being.

Pamper Yourself with Relaxing Baths or Skincare
Indulging in relaxing rituals like baths or skincare routines is a nurturing way to practice self-care. A warm bath infused with essential oils or bath salts soothes tired muscles and calms the mind. Enhance the ambiance with soft music and candles to create a serene escape. Similarly, skincare routines, whether it's applying a facial mask or massaging in a moisturizer, promote physical health and send a message of self-worth. These simple yet luxurious acts of self-pampering remind you to honor your body and create moments of comfort in your day.

Cultivate Gratitude and Self-Compassion
Gratitude and self-compassion are transformative self-care practices that foster emotional resilience. Taking time to reflect on what you're grateful for shifts your perspective, increasing happiness and reducing stress. Journaling, meditating, or simply pausing to appreciate life's blessings strengthens your mental well-being. Equally important is being kind to yourself during challenging times. Practicing self-compassion by offering patience and understanding instead of criticism builds inner strength and peace. Together, gratitude and self-compassion enhance your ability to navigate life's ups and downs with grace and positivity.

Self-care is not a luxury but a necessity for a balanced, fulfilling life. Embrace rituals that resonate with you, and prioritize them regularly. By doing so, you're not only nurturing your body and mind but also cultivating long-term well-being that helps you thrive in every aspect of life.

CONNECT WITH US
www.sherisesstudios.com

REPUTATION AND INTEGRITY IN THE BEAUTY INDUSTRY

by Ashley McCombs

Lemon Ivory Beauty has played a pivotal role in establishing our esteemed reputation within the industry due to its unwavering commitment to excellence and a distinctive approach to luxury hair and makeup services, meticulous attention to detail, combined with a dedication to using the finest products and techniques, ensures that every client experiences a transformative journey that transcends the ordinary.

Moreover, our emphasis on personalized service fosters a deep connection with clients, allowing us to create bespoke beauty experiences that resonate on both aesthetic and emotional levels. This level of customization not only enhances client satisfaction but also encourages word-of-mouth referrals, further solidifying our standing in the competitive landscape.

Additionally, the brand's collaborations with renowned industry professionals and participation in prestigious events have elevated our visibility and credibility. By consistently aligning with the highest standards of artistry and professionalism, which has positioned us as a trusted authority in the luxury beauty sector, attracting discerning clients and establishing a loyal following that contributes to our ongoing success. Success in the beauty industry, hinges on a triad of foundational principles: integrity, excellence, and accountability.

First and foremost, honesty is paramount. In an industry often characterized by trends and fleeting fads, maintaining transparency with clients fosters trust and cultivates a loyal clientele. By openly communicating about services, pricing, and outcomes, we have established ourselves as a reliable partner in each client's beauty journey. This trust is invaluable and can lead to enduring relationships that significantly enhance brand reputation. Delivering exceptional quality in every service is non-negotiable. Our commitment to excellence is reflected not only in the artistry of our services but also in our selection of premium products and techniques.

Consistently exceeding client expectations ensures positive experiences that translate into glowing referrals and repeat business. Lastly, accountability-doing what you say you will do-is crucial in building a reputable brand. Honoring commitments, whether it be

punctuality, delivering on service promises, or following up with clients, it exemplifies professionalism and reliability. This steadfast adherence to our promises reinforces our brand ethos and positions us as a leader in the luxury beauty market.

In essence, by embracing honesty, striving for excellence, and holding ourselves accountable, We can not only thrive in the beauty industry but also set a benchmark for integrity and quality that resonates deeply with our clientele. We're a distinguished luxury bridal hair and makeup company based in Dallas, Texas, renowned for its expertise in creating romantic, soft glam that enhance the natural beauty of each client. Our philosophy centers on the belief that every bride deserves to feel exquisite and confident and we achieve this by utilizing only the highest quality products available in the industry.

We specialize in crafting bespoke beauty experiences tailored to the unique preferences and features of each individual. Prior to the event, we provide personalized skincare consultations and recommendations to ensure that your skin is radiant and prepared for the makeup application. This thoughtful approach underscores our commitment to enhancing not only your external beauty but also your overall well-being. On the day of your event, our dedicated team is by your side, delivering meticulous services that reflect your vision while ensuring longevity and elegance. We understand the importance of flawless presentation, which is why we can remain available for touch-ups during the event, to guarantee that you look and feel your best at every moment. We also offer touch-up kits empowering you to maintain stunning. Whether you envision a romantic bridal style or a sophisticated soft glam appearance, we're committed to making your bridal experience unforgettable, allowing you to embrace your day with grace and confidence.

CONNECT WITH ASHLEY

www.LemonIvoryBeauty.com
Instagram - @LemonIvoryBeauty
Facebook - Lemon Ivory Beauty

THE POWER OF GRATITUDE:
CULTIVATING A THANKFUL HEART FOR BETTER MENTAL AND PHYSICAL HEALTH

In today's fast-paced world, we often find ourselves focused on what we lack or what is yet to be achieved. This constant drive for more can lead to feelings of stress, dissatisfaction, and even burnout. But what if we shifted our perspective? What if, instead of focusing on what is missing, we concentrated on what we already have and expressed gratitude for it? Cultivating a thankful heart has been shown to have profound effects on both mental and physical health, and it can be the key to living a more vibrant and fulfilling life.

The Science of Gratitude

Gratitude is more than just a feel-good emotion; it's a powerful tool that has been proven to improve overall well-being. Research consistently shows that practicing gratitude can reduce stress, increase happiness, and enhance emotional resilience. It activates the brain's reward system, boosting levels of dopamine and serotonin, the neurotransmitters responsible for feelings of joy and contentment. When we express gratitude, our brains release oxytocin, known as the *"love hormone,"* which fosters feelings of connection, trust, and empathy. This is why acts of gratitude—whether giving thanks for a kind gesture or acknowledging the positive aspects of life—can strengthen our relationships and enhance our sense of community. Moreover, gratitude has a tangible impact on our physical health. Studies have found that individuals who regularly practice gratitude experience lower levels of inflammation, improved immune function, and even better sleep quality. Gratitude helps to counteract the negative effects of stress by promoting relaxation and reducing cortisol, the hormone associated with stress.

Gratitude and Mental Health

Mental health is intrinsically linked to our emotional state, and gratitude plays a crucial role in fostering emotional well-being. In moments of hardship or uncertainty, it can be easy to fall into negative thought patterns. However, by choosing to focus on the positive aspects of life—no matter how small—we can break free from this cycle and cultivate a more positive outlook. Gratitude encourages a mindset shift. It allows us to reframe challenges as opportunities for growth and learning, fostering resilience in the face of adversity. By making gratitude a daily practice, individuals can develop a sense of contentment and peace, even during difficult times. For those dealing with anxiety, depression, or other mental health struggles, gratitude can serve as a therapeutic tool. Practicing gratitude exercises, such as keeping a gratitude journal or verbally expressing thanks to others, can help individuals manage negative emotions, enhance self-esteem, and improve their overall mental health.

The Physical Benefits of Gratitude

While the mental health benefits of gratitude are well-documented, its physical benefits are equally impressive. Research shows that people who practice gratitude regularly experience better cardiovascular health, lower blood pressure, and a stronger immune system. These physical benefits are likely due to the reduction of stress hormones and the promotion of a more balanced, peaceful state of mind. Gratitude also has a profound effect on sleep. Many people struggle with insomnia or poor-quality sleep, often due to stress or racing thoughts. Gratitude has been found to improve sleep quality by promoting relaxation and reducing the mental chatter that often keeps us awake at night. A simple practice of reflecting on the positive aspects of the day before bed can lead to a more restful night's sleep.

Furthermore, gratitude has been shown to improve overall health behaviors. People who regularly express gratitude tend to engage in healthier habits, such as exercising more, eating nutritious foods, and getting adequate rest. This is likely because gratitude fosters a sense of self-care and encourages individuals to appreciate their bodies and take better care of them.

Cultivating a Grateful Heart

Now that we know the powerful impact gratitude can have on our lives, the next step is learning how to cultivate a grateful heart. Here are a few simple practices that can help you integrate gratitude into your daily routine:

1. **Keep a Gratitude Journal:** Each day, take a few moments to write down three things you're grateful for. These can be small, everyday occurrences or big moments of joy. Over time, you'll begin to notice how much there is to be thankful for in your life.
2. **Practice Mindfulness:** Mindfulness is the art of being fully present in the moment. By practicing mindfulness, you can become more aware of the simple blessings that surround you every day, from the warmth of the sun to the kindness of a friend.
3. **Express Thanks to Others:** Take the time to thank the people in your life who make a positive impact. Whether it's a friend, family member, colleague, or even a stranger, expressing your gratitude fosters connection and builds stronger relationships.
4. **Reframe Negative Thoughts:** When faced with a challenge, try to reframe the situation by finding something to be grateful for. This shift in perspective can help you stay grounded and focused on solutions, rather than dwelling on problems.
5. **Make Gratitude a Daily Habit:** Just like any other habit, gratitude becomes more powerful the more you practice it. Set aside time each day to reflect on the things you're thankful for, and you'll start to notice a shift in your mindset and overall well-being.

Incorporating gratitude into our daily lives is one of the simplest, yet most effective, ways to improve our mental and physical health. By focusing on what we have rather than what we lack, we can foster a sense of peace, joy, and fulfillment. Whether it's through journaling, mindfulness, or expressing thanks to others, cultivating a grateful heart can unlock a deeper sense of vitality, enhancing our ability to thrive in all areas of life. So, take a moment each day to reflect on the blessings in your life—and let gratitude become the foundation for your health, happiness, and success.

CONNECT WITH US

www.sherisesstudios.com

The SHE RISES STUDIOS PODCAST

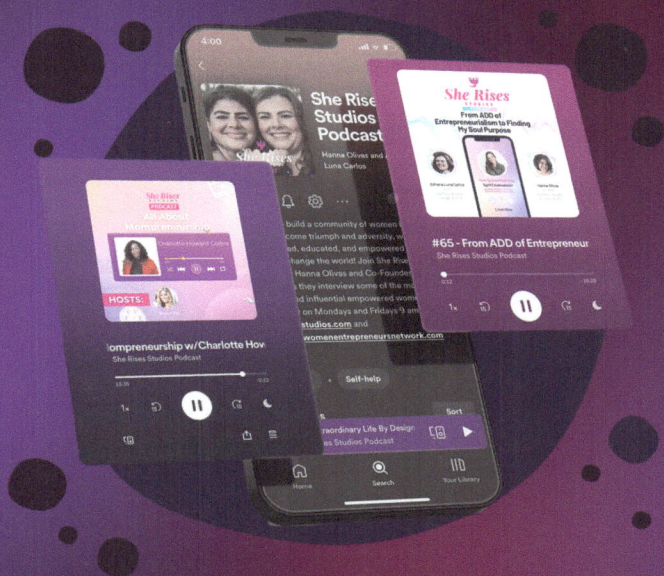

The She Rises Studios podcast is dedicated to empowering women like you to reach their full potential and live their best lives. With inspiring stories, insightful interviews, and practical advice from experts in different industries, our podcast is your go-to source for information, inspiration, and motivation. Join us as we explore topics like:

- Overcoming self-doubt and limiting beliefs
- Building and running a successful business
- Building confidence and Self-esteem
- Navigating career transitions
- Starting and growing a business
- Balancing work and family life
- Improving physical and mental health
- Finding meaning and purpose in life
- So many more

Our guests include successful entrepreneurs, inspiring thought leaders, and everyday women who have overcome challenges and achieved their dreams. Each episode is packed with actionable tips and strategies to help you take your life to the next level.

WALKING FOR WELLNESS: HOW A DAILY WALK CAN PROMOTE HEART HEALTH AND CLEAR THE MIND

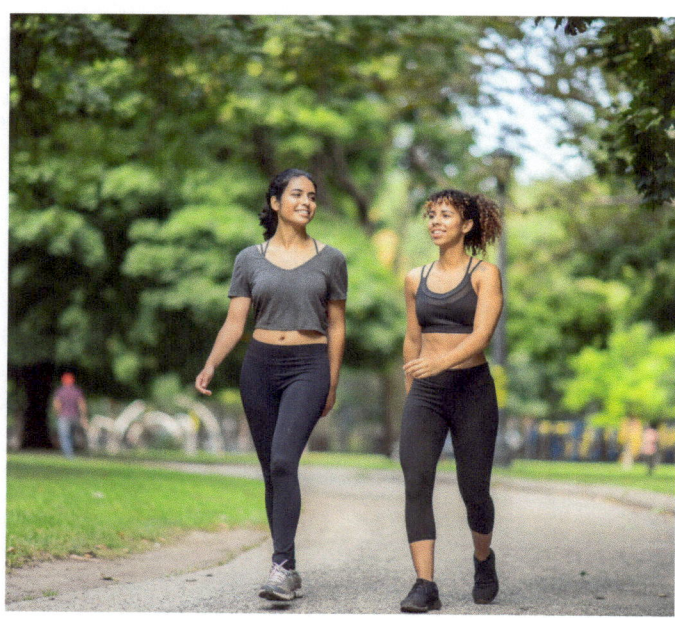

As we juggle multiple responsibilities, we can overlook the small habits that nurture our overall well-being. Yet, one of the easiest and most accessible ways to nurture both your body and mind is through a daily walk. Walking may seem like a basic activity, but its benefits extend far beyond just physical fitness. In this article, we explore how making walking a part of your daily routine can enhance heart health, clear the mind, and contribute to overall well-being.

The Heart-Healthy Benefits of Walking

Your heart, the powerhouse of your body, is critical for your overall health, and maintaining its function is vital for a long, fulfilling life. The American Heart Association recommends physical activity, such as brisk walking, for at least 150 minutes per week. This simple exercise is not only an effective way to improve cardiovascular health but also reduces the risk of heart disease, high blood pressure, and stroke.

When you engage in walking, your heart works more efficiently. The rhythmic motion of walking increases circulation, strengthens the heart, and helps to lower blood pressure. This is due to the way walking helps improve the function of blood vessels, making it easier for your heart to pump blood throughout your body. Over time, regular walking can even lower levels of LDL cholesterol, the *"bad"* cholesterol, while increasing HDL cholesterol, the *"good"* cholesterol, further reducing the risk of heart disease.

Mental Clarity and Stress Relief

A walk offers much more than physical benefits; it's a natural mood booster, too. A daily walk provides time to disconnect from the stresses of daily life, allowing you to clear your mind and alleviate anxiety. Walking releases endorphins, the body's natural *"feel-good"* hormones, which can help reduce stress and elevate mood. As you step away from work or daily tasks, you give yourself the space to think more clearly and gain perspective.

Being outside in nature further enhances this mental clarity. Exposure to natural light and fresh air is beneficial to mental health, reducing feelings of fatigue and boosting energy levels. Whether you walk through a park, along a beach, or just around your neighborhood, nature has the power to recharge you, offering a sense of calm and tranquility that is hard to replicate indoors.

Walking can also be a form of mindfulness. The steady pace, the rhythm of your feet hitting the ground, and the natural sights and sounds around you can help you stay in the present moment. This practice of mindfulness has been shown to reduce negative thoughts and promote a greater sense of calm and balance in your life.

The Mind-Body Connection

Incorporating daily walking into your life strengthens the connection between your body and mind. This simple yet effective exercise allows you to tune into your body's signals, promoting physical awareness and body consciousness. Over time, walking also improves posture, strengthens muscles, and increases flexibility, further benefiting your overall wellness.

Moreover, walking regularly can enhance your sleep quality. Research has shown that physical activity, such as walking, can help regulate sleep patterns, making it easier to fall asleep and stay asleep throughout the night. Better sleep means better recovery for both your body and mind, which contributes to a more balanced and energetic lifestyle.

Making Walking a Part of Your Routine

The beauty of walking is its simplicity. It's an accessible form of exercise that doesn't require expensive equipment or a gym membership. To begin, set a small goal—perhaps a 10-minute walk during your lunch break or an evening stroll after dinner—and gradually build from there. Start with a pace that feels comfortable and gradually challenge yourself to walk faster or longer.

Consistency is key to reaping the benefits of walking. Try to incorporate walking into your daily routine, whether it's walking to work, taking the stairs instead of the elevator, or walking your dog. With each step, you'll improve not just your physical health but also your mental clarity and emotional well-being.

If you're looking to boost your heart health, clear your mind, and embrace a more balanced lifestyle, walking is a powerful and easy way to do so. As part of a holistic approach to well-being, a daily walk can become a small but mighty ritual in your day, offering lasting benefits for both body and mind.

CONNECT WITH US

www.sherisesstudios.com

CHAMPIONING MENTAL HEALTH AND RESILIENCE

by Prudence Hatchett

Prudence Hatchett is a passionate mental health advocate, counselor, and educator dedicated to promoting emotional well-being and resilience. With over a decade of experience in the field, Prudence has worked tirelessly to support individuals in navigating their mental health challenges and fostering a deeper understanding of emotional wellness. Her journey into mental health advocacy began with her own experiences, where she witnessed the profound impact of mental health on individuals and families.

Prudence's approach to counseling is rooted in compassion and empathy. She believes that everyone deserves a safe space to explore their thoughts and feelings, free from judgment. Her therapeutic practice incorporates evidence-based techniques, allowing clients to develop resilience and acquire the skills necessary to manage life's challenges. Prudence understands that mental health is not merely the absence of illness; it encompasses a holistic approach to overall well-being, including physical health, relationships, and personal fulfillment.

In her chapter for Plan A Life You Love, Prudence delves into the importance of mental health awareness and emotional resilience. She emphasizes that mental health is a journey, one that requires ongoing attention and care. Prudence shares practical tools and strategies for cultivating resilience, such as mindfulness practices, cognitive-behavioral techniques, and the importance of self-compassion. Her insights encourage readers to prioritize their mental well-being and recognize that seeking help is a sign of strength.

In addition to her counseling practice, Prudence is committed to community outreach and education. She conducts workshops and training sessions aimed at increasing mental health awareness and promoting emotional well-being. By providing resources and information, Prudence empowers individuals to take charge of their mental health and advocate for themselves and others. Her goal is to create a ripple effect of understanding and support, fostering a culture where mental health is prioritized and stigmas are dismantled.

Through her unwavering dedication to mental health, Prudence Hatchett is making a profound impact on the lives of those she serves. Her belief that everyone deserves the tools to thrive inspires countless individuals to embrace their journey toward emotional wellness. She serves as a guiding light for those seeking support, reminding them that healing is possible and that they are not alone.

GRAB YOUR COPY NOW!

She Stands Strong: 30 Personal Stories of Strength and Resilience is a powerful collection of inspiring narratives that celebrate the triumphs of women who turned their greatest challenges into incredible strengths. Through these personal stories, you'll witness everyday heroes confronting adversity, overcoming setbacks, and embracing vulnerability to transform their lives. This book is a tribute to resilience, a guide to self-discovery, and a beacon of hope, encouraging readers to see challenges not as barriers but as stepping stones toward empowerment.

www.amazon.com/She-Stands-Strong-Personal-Resilience/dp/1964619629

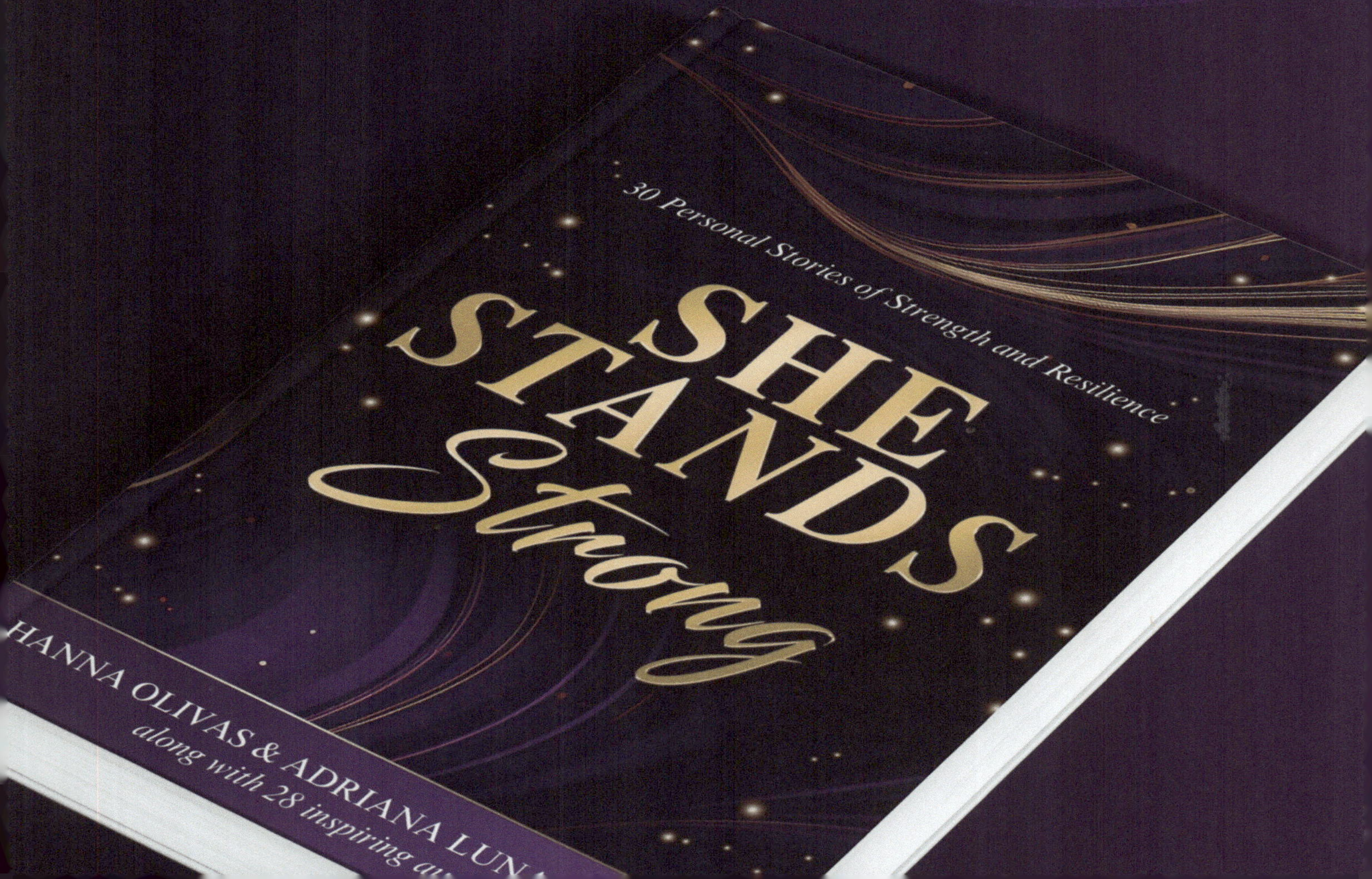

30 Personal Stories of Strength and Resilience

SHE STANDS Strong

HANNA OLIVAS & ADRIANA LUNA
along with 28 inspiring au

CYCLICAL CULTURES

CONNECTING HUMANS+MENOPAUSE
FOR HARMONY IN THE WORKPLACE

🌐 hello@cyclicalcultures.com 📞 250-819-9330

MENOPAUSE IN THE WORKPLACE: HONORING THE NATURAL CYCLE FOR EMPOWERED LEADERSHIP

by Kylye Ralston

Menopause is often seen as a daunting transition—one marked by physical changes, emotional shifts, and a sense of uncertainty. But what if we flipped that script? What if menopause wasn't the end of a chapter, but the start of a new one—one filled with empowerment, leadership, and transformation?

Though difficult, menopause is a transition. Like puberty, it's a temporary phase that leads to something more powerful on the other side. Much like stepping into womanhood, menopause marks a new beginning, where women can emerge with renewed strength and wisdom.

Menopause isn't something to just *"get through."* It can be a moment of release, unraveling the stresses, pain, and silence that many have carried. It's about redefining who we are—reclaiming our voice, stepping into our power, and realizing that our best years are still ahead. It's also a time to connect with something bigger than ourselves. As we move through this phase of life, we are reminded of the natural cycle we are part of—a deeper meaning that calls us to reflect on our purpose and legacy.

Despite how common menopause is, it remains a silent subject in many workplaces. Women often feel they must hide their experiences, fearing judgment. But this silence isn't just personal—it impacts workplaces, relationships, and communities. Today, life and work are no longer separate for many of us. The environments where we spend our time need to foster psychological safety—spaces where the natural phases of our lives, including menopause, are honored and embraced.

More women than ever are seeking leadership roles in their 40s and 50s. But without support, 1 in 10 women leave the workforce due to menopause symptoms, and 25% consider leaving. By creating cultures that value openness and understanding around menopause, we foster environments where women can thrive and contribute fully—not despite menopause, but in partnership with it. We are natural beings going through a natural cycle, and our professional environments should reflect this.

Menopause isn't just a physical journey—it's emotional, mental, and spiritual. It's about stepping into roles that contribute to the world in meaningful ways. This phase of life is where many women find their deepest purpose. The resilience that emerges leads to transformations, not just for ourselves, but for the communities we touch.

The journey through menopause is one of transformation and resilience. It's a chance for every woman to redefine her life on her own terms. When we embrace this natural cycle, in both personal lives and workplaces, we create a future where women feel empowered to lead, to be seen, and to be heard.

This is the mission I've dedicated my work to: ensuring that women everywhere are supported in this phase of life and that workplaces understand the importance of creating cultures of psychological safety. Together, we can ensure no woman feels alone in this journey.

CONNECT WITH KYLYE

www.cyclicalcultures.com
www.linktr.ee/coachkylye
www.linkedin.com/in/coachkylye
www.tiktok.com/@coachkylye
www.youtube.com/@happilyevermenopause

FENIX TV

SHE RISES
STUDIOS

she wins

NICE GIRLS FINISH FIRST

SHE WINS
VIRTUAL SUMMIT 2025

When: May 14–16, 2025
Where: Exclusively on FENIX TV
Tickets: $49.97

Join us for the **She Wins Virtual Summit 2025**, a 3-day event celebrating women entrepreneurs and leaders from around the world. This year's theme, **"Nice Girls Finish First,"** showcases how kindness, empathy, and integrity drive success in business and life.

What to Expect:

- Inspiring stories from women leaders.
- Expert advice on leadership, resilience, and growth.
- Strategies for thriving in business without compromising values.

BE PART OF THIS EMPOWERING MOVEMENT AND DISCOVER HOW KINDNESS LEADS TO GREATNESS!

COMPASSIONATE CHANGE-MAKER AND HOLISTIC WELLNESS ADVOCATE

by MP Montigny

MP Montigny is a dedicated humanitarian whose work transcends borders and cultures. With over a decade of experience serving as an Emergency Coordinator, MP has devoted her life to delivering aid to vulnerable communities facing crises worldwide. Her journey has taken her to challenging environments, including Myanmar, Yemen, and Haiti, where she has witnessed firsthand the impact of compassion and resilience in the face of adversity.

From the outset of her career, MP has understood that true change begins with empathy. Her approach to humanitarian work is grounded in a deep appreciation for the interconnectedness of human experiences. Traveling through over 50 countries, MP has cultivated invaluable insights from diverse cultures, shaping her understanding of holistic well-being and its role in social impact.

In her chapter for Plan A Life You Love, MP shares her philosophy on the importance of selflessness and compassion in making meaningful contributions to the world. She emphasizes that by fostering connections with others and understanding their stories, we can create a ripple effect of positive change. MP believes that each individual has the power to make a difference, and it starts with cultivating empathy within ourselves.

Throughout her career, MP has earned certifications as a Reiki and Tianshi Master, a Beyond Quantum Healer, and a yoga teacher. This holistic approach to well-being informs her work and underscores her belief in the mind-body-spirit connection. She integrates these practices into her humanitarian efforts, encouraging individuals to prioritize their mental and emotional health while contributing to their communities.

MP is also the founder of Anima Mundi Center, an online holistic wellness platform dedicated to inspiring individuals to create a better world by starting with themselves. Through this platform, she offers resources, workshops, and community support aimed at promoting holistic well-being and self-awareness. Her mission is clear: when we nurture our inner selves, we can better serve others.

In her engaging workshops, MP emphasizes the power of inner connection and mindfulness. She encourages participants to explore their emotions, understand their motivations, and recognize their unique contributions to the world. By fostering a sense of community, she helps individuals realize that they are not alone in their journeys, and that together, they can create lasting change.

MP Montigny's commitment to compassion and humanitarianism is both inspiring and transformative. She exemplifies how selflessness and empathy can drive impactful change, reminding us that our actions, no matter how small, can ripple out and influence the world positively. Through her work and advocacy, MP continues to empower individuals to embrace their roles as change-makers, fostering a brighter, more compassionate future for all.

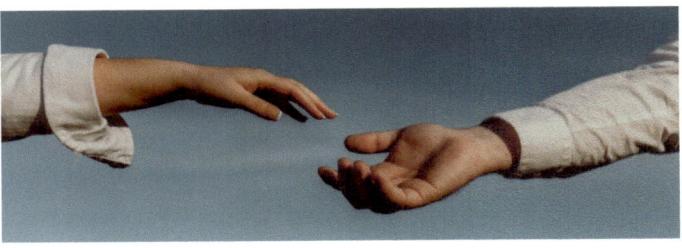

CONNECT WITH MP

www.web.facebook.com/profile.php?
id=100094493185163&_rdc=1&_rdr
www.instagram.com/animamundicenter
www.animamundicenter.com

LISA JACOVSKY: REDEFINING AUTISM THROUGH STORYTELLING

by Lisa Jacovsky

Lisa Jacovsky's journey as an author and advocate is one of profound inspiration, rooted in a deep commitment to changing perceptions of autism. As an award-winning author of ten books, Lisa has built a platform that presents autism in a positive light, drawing from her extensive experience in Applied Behavior Analysis (ABA). Writing has been a dream and a passion for Lisa since she was a child, crafting short stories from the age of seven. Her lifelong love of storytelling laid the foundation for a career dedicated to creating narratives that inspire and uplift.

Lisa's story began over a decade ago when she started working with adults in residential group homes, taking them on enriching monthly outings to places like the Crayola Factory and Dorney Park. These experiences sparked her passion for showing that individuals with autism can enjoy and thrive in diverse environments. However, it was her work with children through in-home ABA that truly ignited her desire to write children's books. Lisa was inspired to create stories that encourage children to befriend those who behave differently, to open up important conversations between kids and their families, and to show that autism does not limit a child's potential. Her books are a testament to this mission, each one highlighting the capabilities of children with autism while addressing various social issues, making her work both impactful and socially relevant.

Lisa's books have garnered praise for their ability to resonate with both children and adults, making them invaluable resources for families, educators, and libraries. Parents and teachers alike have praised the

books for their gentle yet powerful messages that encourage empathy, understanding, and acceptance. Reviews highlight how these stories opened up important conversations in families, helping children to see the beauty in diversity and understand that being different is not something to be feared but celebrated.

One reviewer wrote, *"Lisa Jacovsky's books are a breath of fresh air. They beautifully illustrate how we can all learn to be more accepting and kind, starting from a young age. These are must-have books for any home or school library."* Another reader shared, *"These stories are not just for children with autism but for all children, as they teach life lessons that every child needs to hear. We need more books like these that promote inclusion and understanding."*

Lisa's influence extends beyond her writing. She hosts the award-winning podcast *"No Limits with Lisa Jacovsky,"* where she interviews individuals and organizations making a difference in the world. This podcast has become a platform for sharing stories of resilience, innovation, and hope, further amplifying her mission to foster understanding and acceptance.

Through her podcast, Lisa connected with Brainstorm Productions, a pioneering company that employs individuals with autism in animation and illustration. Recognizing their incredible talent, Lisa collaborated with Brainstorm Productions to illustrate four of her books, with two more projects planned for 2025. This collaboration exemplifies Lisa's dedication to creating opportunities for individuals with autism to showcase their creative gifts. Her work is not just about storytelling—it's about fostering understanding, inclusion, and empowerment for those on the autism spectrum.

Lisa Jacovsky's journey is a powerful reminder that everyone has a unique story to tell and that with compassion, creativity, and determination, we can change the narrative around autism. Through her books and podcast, Lisa continues to inspire, educate, and advocate, making a lasting impact on the lives of children and families around the world. Her books are more than just stories—they are tools for building a more inclusive and compassionate future, making them essential additions to the shelves of families, schools, and libraries everywhere.

10 Beautiful books with a message

CONNECT WITH LISA

diverseinkbooks.my.canva.site
fb: booksbylisajacovsky
instagram: diverseinkbooks
tiktok: lisajayauthor18

JOIN OUR COMMUNITY

We believe the future is female and that we are better and stronger together. This group is NOT just for entrepreneurs but for women in general of all ages and from all walks of life.

www.bit.ly/srscommunitygroup

WE ARE
SHE RISES STUDIOS

We are a real-life community of women working to become the best version of themselves to change their lives and make the world a better place.

Group by **Hanna J Olivas**

She Rises Studios Community

🔒 Private group · 6.4K members

+ Invite   ↱ Share   👥 Joined ▾   ▾

Discussion   Featured   Members   Events   Media   Files   🔍   ⋯

Write something...   **About**

THE ART OF SAYING NO: PROTECTING YOUR ENERGY FOR BETTER MENTAL WELL-BEING

As we navigate a society that thrives on constant busyness and the desire to satisfy everyone around us, it's easy to lose sight of our own limits and personal well-being. Whether it's an invitation, a work task, or a favor for a friend, saying *"yes"* has become a reflex rather than a thoughtful decision. However, the key to nurturing your mental well-being may be simpler than we realize—the power of saying no.

We live in a society that celebrates multitasking and endless availability, but this constant state of engagement can leave us feeling depleted and disconnected from our own needs. Learning the art of saying no is not about rejection or negativity—it's about honoring your personal boundaries, preserving your energy, and taking control of what you give attention to. It's about creating space for what truly aligns with your priorities and mental health.

In this article, we delve into the profound benefits of setting boundaries through the simple act of saying no, and how this practice can contribute to improved emotional and mental well-being. By learning to protect your time and energy, you can cultivate a more balanced and fulfilling life.

Understanding the Need to Set Boundaries

Saying no can be uncomfortable, especially for those who pride themselves on being helpful, dependable, or agreeable. We've all experienced moments when we overcommit ourselves out of a sense of obligation or guilt. However, each time we say yes to something that drains our energy or doesn't align with our priorities, we say no to ourselves. This quiet sacrifice can lead to burnout, resentment, and an inability to focus on the things that truly matter to us.

Setting boundaries is a healthy act of self-care. It's recognizing that your time and energy are valuable and finite resources, and you have the right to use them in ways that nurture your physical, emotional, and mental well-being.

The Benefits of Saying No for Mental Health

1. Reduces Stress and Anxiety

When we say yes to everything, we take on more than we can manage. This not only causes stress but also fuels anxiety about deadlines, obligations, and unfulfilled expectations. By saying no, you create space to focus on the tasks that are most important to you, reducing the mental clutter and pressure that come from overcommitting.

2. Fosters Self-Respect and Confidence

Every time you honor your own boundaries, you reinforce a sense of self-respect. Saying no empowers you to take control of your choices and act in alignment with your own values. This practice strengthens your confidence, as you begin to trust your intuition and realize that you are worthy of prioritizing your needs.

3. Promotes Emotional Well-Being

Overloading yourself with commitments can lead to emotional exhaustion and burnout. Saying no helps to protect your emotional reserves, allowing you to give your best self to the people and causes that matter most to you. By not overextending yourself, you create space for joy, relaxation, and positive experiences.

4. Improves Focus and Productivity

When you say no to distractions and unnecessary commitments, you free up mental bandwidth for the things that truly require your attention. This focused energy leads to better decision-making, increased productivity, and a deeper sense of satisfaction in the tasks you choose to take on.

How to Say No Without Guilt

The idea of saying no can bring up feelings of guilt, especially for those who have been conditioned to please others. But it's important to recognize that setting boundaries is a form of self-respect, not selfishness. Here are a few ways to say no gracefully:

1. Be Direct and Honest

Instead of offering vague excuses, be straightforward and honest about your reasons. A simple, *"I'm unable to take this on right now due to other commitments"* is both clear and respectful. People will appreciate your honesty, and you'll feel empowered by your ability to communicate your limits.

2. Offer an Alternative (When Appropriate)

If you're comfortable, you can offer an alternative solution. For example, *"I can't attend the meeting, but I'd be happy to review the notes afterward."* This shows that you're still willing to contribute while honoring your boundaries.

3. Use "I" Statements

To avoid sounding dismissive or ungrateful, use *"I"* statements that focus on your needs. For example, *"I need to take some time for myself this weekend"* is a powerful way to communicate that you are prioritizing your well-being.

4. Practice Saying No

The more you practice saying no, the easier it becomes. Start with small, low-stakes situations, and gradually work your way up to more significant commitments. With time, you'll become more comfortable with the process and less likely to feel guilty.

Ultimately, saying no is a form of self-love and protection. It allows you to conserve your energy and direct it toward the people, activities, and projects that align with your values and aspirations. When you learn to prioritize yourself, you become better equipped to serve others and show up as your best self.

So, next time you're faced with a request that doesn't serve your well-being, remember that it's okay to say no. By doing so, you're making room for more meaningful experiences, cultivating mental clarity, and nurturing the kind of life that truly nourishes your soul.

CONNECT WITH US

www.sherisesstudios.com

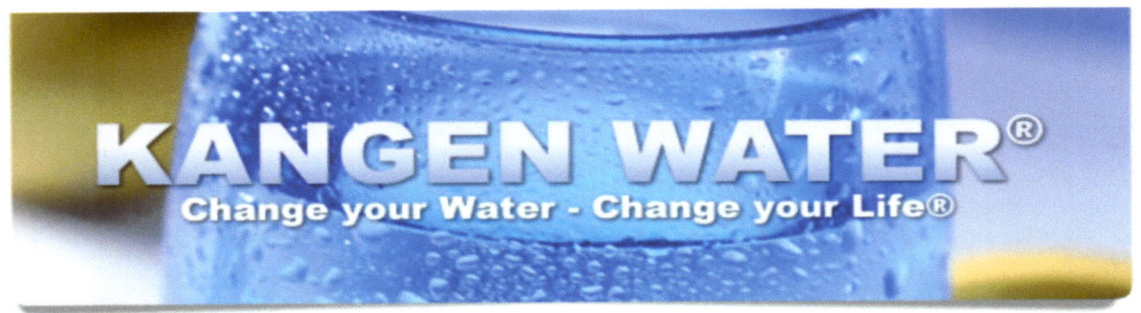

Why Should You Drink Water?

You have probably heard that water makes up over 70% of the body, right? Water is part of all body fluids and is vital to the proper function of the body's organ systems. It should be obvious then that the quality of the water you drink is extremely important. For your body to be at optimal health, you should drink only the purest and cleanest water possible.

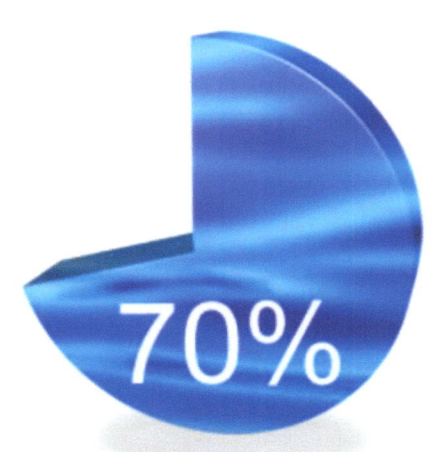

**For more information, email
MyDailyWaterforHealth@gmail.com**

Get your Kangen Water® System TODAY!

The Kangen Alkaline Ionized Water System is compact and easy to install in any home or office. It will conveniently transform your tap water into healthy, balanced water that is perfect for your lifestyle and your wellness goals.

MELISSA FERRER-BURKE: EMPOWERING WOMEN THROUGH ART AND HEALING AT ELLEVATE HER

by Melissa Ferrer-Burke

In a world where art meets healing, Melissa Ferrer-Burke stands as a visionary leader, passionately dedicated to empowering women through the transformative power of creative expression. As the CEO and *"Visionary-in-Chief"* of **Ellevate Her**, a healing center and foundation launched in 2023, Melissa has cultivated a sanctuary for women to thrive, offering programs that focus on recovery, self-discovery, and personal growth. With a lifetime of personal experience and artistic exploration, Melissa has crafted an environment where art, therapy, and holistic wellness come together to foster healing for single women.

Melissa's journey is one marked by resilience and the determination to turn her personal experiences into something meaningful for others. A trauma survivor herself, she is no stranger to the complexities of healing, and it is this profound understanding that drives her commitment to supporting women on their paths to recovery. *"I passionately believe in the transformative power of the arts to empower women. Throughout my life, I have dedicated myself to supporting women, channeling my own experiences and artistic vision into meaningful action,"* she explains.

The Creation of Ellevate Her: A Lifelong Vision Realized
In the fall of 2023, Melissa launched Ellevate Her, a foundation based in Florida that is more than just a center for healing; it is a sanctuary where women can come together in a nurturing community to learn, grow, and express themselves. For Melissa, the timing of the foundation's launch was deeply personal and symbolic. She attributes much of the center's creation to what she refers to as *"divine timing,"* where all of her life's experiences, education, and global exposure

came together at the right moment to serve others. *"All of my life's experiences and education were able to come together at this time to help others along their healing paths,"* she says, reflecting on the foundation's beginnings.

A Lifetime of Learning and Mentorship
Melissa's journey to becoming a leader in healing and empowerment didn't happen overnight. She acknowledges the importance of mentorship and guidance in her life, having studied healing programs, wellness retreats, and artistic workshops around the world. Each of these experiences was pivotal in shaping the programs offered at Ellevate Her. From art therapy to yoga, breathwork, and even cold plunging, every modality has been personally explored by Melissa on her own path to healing. *"Every program we offer at EH I have personally studied, used, and found helpful along my personal journey,"* she shares. This hands-on approach ensures that the women at Ellevate Her receive authentic, effective support.

Art as a Path to Healing
At the heart of Ellevate Her lies the belief that art can be a powerful tool for healing. The center offers a variety of art therapy sessions designed to provide women with a safe space to express their emotions without the need for words. *"Art therapy can provide a safe environment for authentic expression, an opportunity to 'verbalize' inner emotions without having to talk, can help contain overwhelming emotions, and help reconcile negative feelings,"* Melissa explains. The creative process allows women to connect with their innermost selves, using artistic expression as a means of self-discovery and emotional healing.

The *"Rise, Melissa"* Art Series: A Collaborative Journey of Transformation

Melissa's personal journey of resilience and empowerment is perhaps most vividly captured in her art series, *"Rise, Melissa."* This collection of six artworks is a collaborative effort between Melissa and world-renowned photographer Robert Farber, with whom she has shared both a personal and professional relationship for over 25 years. Their creative partnership, which began in 1999, has produced a body of work that seamlessly blends photography and painting to tell a compelling narrative of transformation.

"Combining my true emotion and his elegant lens, we were able to connect sight and feeling as subject and photographer," Melissa reflects on the collaboration. The *"Rise, Melissa"* series takes viewers on a powerful journey of growth, resilience, and self-discovery, using vivid colors and evocative imagery to convey the emotional experiences Melissa has encountered throughout her life.

Building a Community of Empowerment

While art is central to the work at Ellevate Her, Melissa believes that the true strength of the foundation lies in its community. *"You're only as strong as your team. In one word, community,"* she emphasizes. The center is designed to be a supportive environment where women can heal and grow together. The women at Ellevate Her come from diverse backgrounds, but they are united by a shared mission of healing and empowerment.

The success of the foundation's programs is a testament to Melissa's holistic approach. Whether it's through art therapy, life coaching, or physical practices like yoga and breathwork, the programs at Ellevate Her are tailored to each individual. *"Each individual is unique. We at EH are proud to say that we cater programs to each specific case,"* Melissa explains. This personalized approach has led to life-changing transformations for many of the women who have participated.

The Power of Collaboration and Knowledge Sharing

For Melissa, collaboration is key to creating a thriving community. She believes that every woman has unique skills and experiences to offer, and that by learning from one another, they can become stronger. *"Knowledge is power. We all have such a unique set of skills. We learn from each other and are always stronger together and united,"* she says.

Melissa's dedication to this philosophy extends beyond the walls of Ellevate Her. She envisions the foundation as a global movement, connecting women from around the world who share a common goal of healing and personal expansion. Already, she is working to bridge her home base in South Florida with Florence, Italy, providing opportunities for international education and collaboration.

Looking to the Future

As Ellevate Her continues to grow, Melissa's vision for the future is expansive. *"I see EH building centers globally,"* she says, envisioning a network of healing centers that empower women worldwide. Her goal is to create spaces where women can connect, heal, and learn from one another, transcending geographical boundaries to build a global sisterhood of support and empowerment.

Through her unwavering dedication, Melissa Ferrer-Burke is not only transforming the lives of the women she serves, but also demonstrating the profound impact that art and community can have on the healing process. Ellevate Her is a reflection of her life's work—an ongoing journey of resilience, empowerment, and creativity that continues to inspire women to rise to their fullest potential.

CONNECT WITH MELISSA
www.instagram.com/ellevate_her
www.linkedin.com/company/ellevate-her/about
www.ellevateher.org

Photo Credits: Rosina Di Bello
@rosinadibellophoto

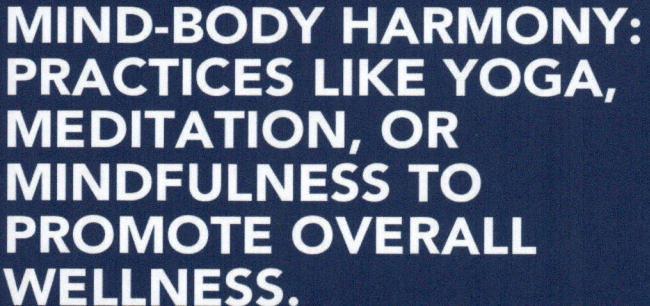

MIND-BODY HARMONY: PRACTICES LIKE YOGA, MEDITATION, OR MINDFULNESS TO PROMOTE OVERALL WELLNESS.

In today's fast-paced world, the connection between the mind and body is often overlooked. Yet, this harmony is essential for achieving overall wellness. Practices like yoga, meditation, and mindfulness are more than just trends—they are time-tested tools that help balance mental clarity with physical vitality, fostering a sense of inner peace and resilience.

Mind-body harmony isn't about perfection; it's about creating a state of balance where your thoughts, emotions, and actions align with your well-being. By incorporating mindful practices into your daily routine, you can unlock the potential for improved health, reduced stress, and greater emotional stability.

1. Yoga: Uniting Mind, Body, and Spirit
Yoga is a centuries-old practice that combines physical postures, breathing techniques, and meditation to promote mental and physical well-being.
- **Improve Flexibility and Strength:** The poses, or asanas, in yoga help improve muscle strength, posture, and flexibility, reducing the risk of injury and chronic pain.
- **Enhance Mental Clarity:** The focus on breathing and movement creates a meditative state that calms the mind and reduces anxiety.
- **Accessible for All:** From beginners to advanced practitioners, yoga offers a variety of styles—like Hatha, Vinyasa, or Yin yoga—that cater to individual needs and preferences.

2. Meditation: Finding Stillness in a Busy World
Meditation is the practice of focusing your mind to achieve a state of calm and heightened awareness.
- **Reduce Stress and Anxiety:** Regular meditation lowers cortisol levels, helping you feel more centered and less overwhelmed.
- **Boost Mental Focus:** Meditation sharpens concentration, improving productivity and decision-making.
- **Cultivate Gratitude:** Practices like loving-kindness meditation encourage positive thinking and emotional resilience.

For beginners, even five minutes of meditation each day can make a noticeable difference in your mental state.

3. Mindfulness: Living Fully in the Present
Mindfulness is the art of paying attention to the present moment without judgment. It's about embracing life as it unfolds, rather than getting caught up in past regrets or future worries.

- **Mindful Breathing:** Simply focusing on your breath can anchor your thoughts and bring a sense of calm during stressful moments.
- **Mindful Eating:** By savoring each bite, you can foster a deeper connection with your food and prevent overeating.

- **Mindful Movement:** Activities like walking or stretching can become meditative when you focus on the sensations in your body and the rhythm of your movements.

4. Combining Practices for Maximum Wellness
While each of these practices offers unique benefits, combining them can amplify their impact on your well-being. For example:
- Begin your day with a 10-minute yoga session to awaken your body and mind.
- Dedicate a few moments to meditation during lunch to refocus your energy.
- Practice mindfulness in the evening, reflecting on the day's moments without judgment.

5. The Science of Mind-Body Harmony
Research supports the transformative power of these practices:
- Studies show that yoga improves heart health, reduces inflammation, and boosts immunity.
- Meditation has been linked to better mental health, increased empathy, and enhanced memory.
- Mindfulness reduces stress, improves sleep quality, and fosters a greater sense of life satisfaction.

By engaging in these practices consistently, you can enhance not only your physical and mental health but also your emotional well-being.

6. Tips to Get Started
If you're new to yoga, meditation, or mindfulness, here's how to begin:
- **Start Small:** Dedicate just 5-10 minutes daily to any of these practices.
- **Find Resources:** Use apps, online classes, or local instructors to guide you through the basics.
- **Be Patient:** Progress takes time. Celebrate small milestones along the way.
- **Create a Routine:** Integrate these practices into your daily life, whether it's starting your morning with yoga or ending your day with a meditation session.

7. Embrace the Journey
Mind-body harmony is a journey, not a destination. As you explore these practices, you'll discover new ways to nurture yourself and cultivate a deeper connection between your mind and body. Achieving overall wellness doesn't require drastic changes. Instead, it's about integrating mindful moments into your daily routine. By prioritizing yoga, meditation, or mindfulness, you're not just promoting harmony—you're investing in a healthier, more balanced version of yourself. Let these practices guide you toward a life of vitality, clarity, and inner peace. Your journey to mind-body harmony starts today.

PRIORITIZE SELF-CARE TO THRIVE: INSIGHTS FROM JENNIFER & NATASHA

by Jennifer Griffith and Natasha Ganes

In today's fast-paced world, stress has become an unavoidable part of life. However, prolonged stress can lead to burnout, affecting our mental, physical, and emotional well-being. Jennifer Griffith and Natasha Ganes, co-creators of *"In the Life of Zen"* and hosts of the "Where Money Meets Soul" podcast, understand the importance of prioritizing self-care to avoid burnout and thrive in every aspect of life.

Drawing from their combined expertise in health, wellness, and professional development, Jennifer and Natasha offer valuable insights into the transformative power of self-care. Through their own personal journeys, they have discovered the profound impact that prioritizing self-care can have on overall well-being.

Natasha's Story resonates with many individuals who find themselves juggling multiple responsibilities and struggling to manage stress effectively. As a busy woman with numerous commitments, Natasha understands the challenges of balancing career, family, and personal goals. At one point, stress consumed her life, leaving her overwhelmed and exhausted. However, through prioritizing self-care, Natasha was able to regain control of her life and find fulfillment.

Similarly, Jennifer's Story highlights the dangers of neglecting self-care in pursuit of productivity. As someone who thrives on constant activity and achievement, Jennifer found herself on the brink of burnout after years of relentless work. Recognizing the importance of self-care, Jennifer embarked on a journey of self-discovery and transformation, reclaiming her health and happiness in the process.

Stress, overwhelm, and burnout are common experiences in today's society, but Jennifer and Natasha emphasize the importance of recognizing the signs and taking proactive steps to prioritize self-care. By incorporating self-care practices into daily routines, individuals can protect their mental and physical health, enhance productivity, and cultivate a greater sense of well-being.

To avoid burnout and thrive in life, Jennifer and Natasha offer practical tips for prioritizing self-care:

1. **Write Down Everything You Need to Do and Learn to Delegate:** By creating a list of tasks and prioritizing them, individuals can identify areas where they can delegate or eliminate tasks that are not essential.
2. **Accept Your Emotions and Change Your Perspective:** Instead of dwelling on negative thoughts and emotions, practice gratitude and focus on positive aspects of life.

3. **Create Boundaries and Stick with Them:** Learn to say no to commitments that are not aligned with your priorities, and establish healthy boundaries to protect your time and energy.
4. **Exercise:** Incorporate regular physical activity into your routine to reduce stress, boost mood, and improve overall health.
5. **Practice Mindfulness:** Take time to quiet the mind and focus on the present moment through meditation, deep breathing, or other mindfulness practices.
6. **Try Something New:** Step out of your comfort zone and engage in activities that bring joy and fulfillment, whether it's learning a new hobby or exploring new experiences.
7. **Take a Digital Detox:** Disconnect from electronic devices periodically to reduce screen time and promote relaxation.
8. **Meditate:** Set aside time for meditation or guided relaxation to calm the mind and reduce stress.
9. **Prioritize Sleep:** Ensure adequate rest by establishing a bedtime routine and creating a conducive sleep environment.

By incorporating these self-care practices into daily life, individuals can protect their well-being, enhance resilience, and unlock their full potential. Jennifer and Natasha's message is clear: prioritizing self-care is not selfish; it's essential for living a balanced, fulfilling life.

Through their platform, *"In the Life of Zen,"* Jennifer and Natasha share their experiences and insights to empower others to prioritize self-care and create the life of their dreams. By embracing self-care as a non-negotiable aspect of life, individuals can cultivate greater happiness, resilience, and overall well-being.

In the journey of life, self-care is the key to unlocking our full potential and living with purpose and passion. With Jennifer and Natasha's guidance, individuals can embark on a transformative journey of self-discovery, empowerment, and holistic well-being.

CONNECT WITH JENNIFER AND NATASHA

www.instagram.com/inthelifeofzen
www.facebook.com/inthelifeofzen
www.linkedin.com/company/53218206/admin
www.inthelifeofzen.com

Clean Beauty

"FACELIFT IN A BOTTLE" A replenishing face serum that erases fine lines, smoothes wrinkles, refreshes collagen & soothes sensitive skin! Because you only get one chance with your face in this lifetime!

WWW.DRMONICASNATURALBEAUTY.COM

f www.facebook.com/drmonicasbeautyandselfcare

in www.linkedin.com/in/dr-monica-riley-708524174

○ www.instagram.com/drmonicabickerstaffriley

MINH VU: A JOURNEY OF HOLISTIC HEALING AND MIRACLES

Minh Vu, CEO, and founder of Endotransformation, has emerged as a beacon of hope and inspiration for women battling endometriosis and infertility. Through her own firsthand experience with stage 4 endometriosis and infertility, Minh has not only overcome immense challenges but has also defied the odds by naturally conceiving twin boys. Her journey from pain and despair to healing and joy serves as a testament to the power of holistic health and the resilience of the human spirit.

In her chapter, *"Light & The Protective Warrior,"* Minh shares poignant lessons learned from her journey, each narrated from a unique perspective that captures the depth of her experiences.

Lesson #1: Be Your Own Health Advocate
Minh's journey began with three years of unsuccessful attempts to conceive, culminating in a diagnosis of stage 4 endometriosis. Devastated by the news of infertility, Minh embarked on a quest to reclaim her health and fertility through holistic means. With unwavering determination, she committed to being her own health advocate, embracing a holistic lifestyle that ultimately restored balance to her body and alleviated her chronic pain. Through this transformative journey, Minh discovered the power of self-advocacy and the importance of trusting her intuition in navigating her health challenges.

Lesson #2: God Still Performs Miracles
Amidst the turmoil of infertility and endometriosis, Minh and her husband Tom experienced the miraculous joy of conceiving twin boys. Their journey, however, was fraught with challenges, including complications such as Twin-to-Twin Transfusion Syndrome (TTTS) and placental abruption. Through moments of fear and uncertainty, Minh and Tom remained steadfast in their faith, believing in the possibility of miracles. Their sons, Luke and Liam, became symbols of resilience and hope, embodying the transformative power of love and faith in the face of adversity.

Lesson #3: Keep the Faith
Throughout her journey, Minh confronted fears of inadequacy, rejection, and hopelessness, ultimately finding solace in faith and self-discovery. Embracing her inner strength and resilience, Minh learned to overcome obstacles with grace and determination. Her message of hope and empowerment resonates deeply with women battling similar challenges, offering a beacon of light in the darkest of times.

Minh's journey serves as a powerful reminder that healing is possible, even in the face of seemingly insurmountable obstacles. Through her work at Endotransformation, Minh continues to empower women to advocate for their own health and embrace holistic healing. Her message of resilience, faith, and empowerment inspires countless individuals to embrace their own journeys of healing and transformation.

CONNECT WITH MINH

www.instagram.com/endotransformation
www.linkedin.com/in/endotransformation
www.facebook.com/groups/endotransformation
www.endotransformation.com

YOUR GOAL IS ONE STEP AWAY

by *Tammy Cameron*

Put one foot in front of the other. Do it again. Celebrate you!

Life presents many choices. It is up to us to lead, participate, or sit out an experience. The decision is not as important as the alignment with our feeling. We all have our seasons of active participation and of quiet reflection. When we make a decision and our core is screaming something different, this is where we self-sabotage ourselves. Are we sitting out an experience because we are afraid, because we do not want to disappoint someone, or because society tells us it is not the right action or the right time? Are we worried about regrets, misfortune, or potential calamity, doubting our own ability to make the best choice? Are we overextending ourselves saying *'yes'* to everything when deep down we know we desperately need rest? Are we stuck in a stage of gathering information and not feeling quite ready? Are we simply overwhelmed by so many choices? Stop. Breathe. Listen.

In a quiet village, exploring the sights, enjoying the life of a tourist, soaking up the sunshine, I walked through the street with two friends. The vegetation was lush, the cobblestone path was welcoming, and the road led to one spot – the entrance to a trail up a mountain. What was absent from this moment was the stress of a packed work schedule and memories of emergency hospital visits and operations. What was ahead was adventure and I wanted that adventure. One friend agreed; the other did not. This was a huge quandary for me, wanting consensus, wanting to please both parties, and wanting to be true to myself at the same time. In the end, I put myself first, a life lesson that has taken time to learn.

I was ill-prepared to climb a mountain, dressed in high-heeled sandals. Nevertheless, the climbing experience called to me. The climb up was exhilarating and breathtaking. I navigated a winding path upward.

I met vendors along the way, selling handmade jewelry along with raw and polished stones, all small items that they had carefully selected and carried up with them. I admired both the workmanship and their dedication.

Finally, the heat took a toll and fatigue set in about three quarters of the way up. Nevertheless, I had started that climb to reach the top, not to stop. I rested. I drank water. I imagined the view from the top. I began again. The view at the top was spectacular! The sun was beaming gloriously. The homes and businesses below were tranquil from such a distance. The air was fresh and all of the tourists at the top were basking in their triumph. Hello, Tepoztlán! You are etched in my heart.

Put one foot in front of the other. Repeat. Celebrate. This was my choice. I could have stayed paralyzed in indecision, afraid to disappoint someone or deciding I was not prepared with my high-heeled sandals, and time would have passed by. I could have wallowed in my concern about some imagined emergency that could have happened along the way. Instead, I decided to listen.

Stop. Breathe. Listen. What does your core being want to do in this moment? What is stopping you? Allow yourself the time, space, and opportunity to celebrate your unstoppable self.

Stumble in imperfection along the path to your goal. I certainly stumbled on that mountain, tripping on tree roots along the way; I do not regret a moment of the experience. You deserve your mountain-top! Step forward with one foot. Repeat. Say *'yes'* to you!

CONNECT WITH TAMMY

www.calmstrategy.ca
www.facebook.com/Calm.Strategy
www.instagram.com/tammystma

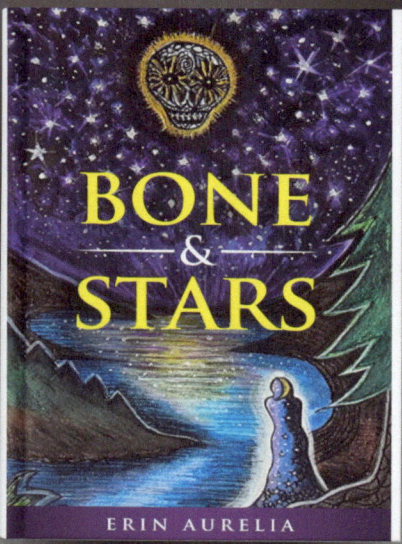

BONE & STARS
by Erin Aurelia

Bone & Stars is a powerful poetry collection that traces one woman's journey from silence and emotional abuse to liberation and self-reclamation. These poems delve into the raw determination to truly live—not as someone numbed by denial, but as a whole, defiant, and shining self. Through vivid, unflinching verses, the author explores escaping an abusive marriage, healing unseen wounds, and finding her voice to rise like a phoenix, unapologetic and fierce.

This collection offers solace and recognition to those who have endured emotional abuse, providing a mirror for experiences often dismissed because they leave no visible scars. It is a testament to the resilience of the spirit and a reminder that recovery and self-empowerment are possible. Bone & Stars is an anthem for anyone seeking to break free, heal, and shine as the center of their own universe.

HEALING JOURNAL FOR WARRIOR WOMEN
by Marika Wessels

Healing Journal for Warrior Women is your companion for growth, resilience, and self-discovery. Designed to empower your journey, this guided journal combines mindfulness exercises, reflective prompts, and uplifting affirmations to help you navigate challenges, embrace your inner strength, and cultivate self-love. Whether you're healing from past wounds, reclaiming your voice, or seeking balance, this journal provides the tools and inspiration to transform pain into power. Let this be your safe space to reflect, recharge, and rise as the warrior woman you are.

AVAILABLE ON AMAZON

amazon

PUBLISHED BY SHE RISES STUDIOS
www.SheRisesStudios.com

THE POWER OF PUBLISHING
WHY PUBLISH A BOOK, YOU ASK?

Publishing a book is one of the most fulfilling ways to share your story with the world and leave a lasting legacy. It boosts your credibility and highlights your expertise in your industry. Plus, you'll be stepping into the massive $138.5 billion book market industry —and it's still growing!

Best of all, it's easier now than ever before to get your book out there. How exciting is that?

At She Rises Studios, we are on a mission to become the top publishing house for women in the USA. We believe in the power of storytelling to create influencers and stronger communities. We're here to help you break barriers, grow, and make waves in the publishing world.

Get published with us TODAY!

Visit *www.SheRisesStudios.com* or email us at
contact@sherisesstudios.com